Recovering
FROM
CHURCHES
THAT
ABUSE

Recovering
FROM
CHURCHES
THAT
ABUSE

RONALD ENROTH

ZondervanPublishingHouse
Grand Rapids, Michigan

A Division of HarperCollins*Publishers*

Recovering from Churches That Abuse
Copyright © 1994 by Ronald M. Enroth

Address inquiries to:
  Zondervan Publishing House,
  Grand Rapids, Michigan 49530.

Enroth, Ronald M.
      Recovering from Churches that abuse/Ronald Enroth.
        p.   cm.
      Companion to: Churches that abuse.
      Includes bibliological references and index.
      ISBN 0-310-39870-3 (alk. paper)
      1. Church work with ex-cultists. 2. Ex-cultists—Religious
life. 3. Ex-cultists—Pastoral counseling of. 4. Enroth, Ronald
M. Churches that abuse. 5. Control (Psychology)—Religious aspects—Chrisitianity.   I. Enroth, Ronald M. Churches that
abuse. II. Title.
BV4460.55.E67   1994
259'.08'69—dc20   94-13553
                                                                 CIP

International trade paperback edition ISBN 0-310-39877-0

All Scripture quotations, unless otherwise indicated, are taken
from the Holy Bible: New International Version®. NIV®. Copyright
© 1973, 1978, 1984 by International Bible Society. Used by permission of Zondervan Publishing House. All rights reserved.

Printed in the United States of America

94 95 96 97 98 /❖ DH / 10 9 8 7 6 5 4 3 2 1

This edition is printed on acid-free paper and meets the Ameri-
can National Standards Institute Z39.48 standard.

Dedicated to all those hurting Christians who thought nobody cared or understood. You are not alone.

Contents

Preface

In the chapters that follow you will be introduced to many people: Carlos, Cecily, Steve and Bridget, Peter, and Alan among others. They are people who have experienced varying degrees of spiritual abuse and have achieved varying levels of recovery. Although I am a sociologist, the research for this book is not based on questionnaires or surveys. No statistics or percentiles are included. I do not even claim that the narratives found here are a "representative sample" in the technical, methodological sense even though I have tried to present typical accounts of spiritual and emotional abuse.

The information presented here is based on many informal, in-depth interviews, correspondence, and telephone conversations with dozens of former members of different churches that abuse. More than anything, I want to convey as well as I can the personal accounts of these people in the hope that I can persuade a few readers that some churches do hurt people and that it is possible to recover from such abuse.

In short, I hope to allow the victims of abuse to speak their own thoughts and tell their own stories, which I have edited and put into narrative form, interrupting them from time to time with my comments and the insights of other writers. I have disguised names except in a few instances in which the respondents specifically requested that I use their actual names. With one or two exceptions, I use the real names of the churches involved. In some cases I have merged the experiences of several former members and present a composite picture.

My primary purpose in this book is to describe the processes of recovery, the obstacles encountered on the way, and the factors that inhibit or retard a satisfactory recovery. To that end I have tried to be selective in the details I relate about the abusive church experiences, choosing those that seem to me to have the most profound influence on the process of a victim's recovery. The kinds of experiences I relate are described in more detail in the forerunner to this book, *Churches That Abuse.*

Moreover, I do not attempt to suggest a one-two-three process of recovery. As you will see, the road to recovery is different for each person; there is no prescriptive formula to follow or predictable pattern. Some of the people you will meet are still traveling that hazardous road. Yet you will be able to discern recurring themes and problems, which I believe offer tangible clues about recovery to victims, their families, their friends, and their counselors.

People who have been abused are often not believed or taken seriously. One former member, Shawn Haugh, described the problem this way: "One of the most painful feelings I have had in the recovery process is the damage to my self-esteem caused by having what I say and think ignored. It feels like being erased as unimportant, like I don't matter or don't count. But I do. I exist and I am real. These things happened to me, a person with a name, a face, feelings, and a life. My hope is that you will lend me and other ex-members your voice."[1]

In this book I seek to be the voice of the voiceless, and I hope that in listening, you will learn and be warned and find hope for recovery from churches that abuse.

Acknowledgments

I am grateful to the many people who consented to be interviewed for this book. To many, I was a stranger and you trusted me. I hope that trust is rewarded in these pages. I wish it were possible to tell everyone's personal story, but in a sense this is everyone's story.

I am especially grateful to my daughter, Kara Bettencourt, without whose considerable editing and computer skills this book would not have been possible. And thanks to her husband, Jerome, for his understanding and suggestions.

Thanks to the administration of Westmont College for granting me a half-year's sabbatical to complete the manuscript.

To those who helped along the way, thanks to Betty Fleming, Ned Divelbiss, Herb and Louise Moeller, my student assistants, and most of all, my wife, Ruth-Anne.

Finally, thanks to Jim Ruark, Rachel Boers, Shauna Perez, and their associates at Zondervan Publishing House who patiently waited and then helped turn a manuscript and computer disks into a book. Thanks in advance to the marketing and media people at Zondervan for their outstanding work, and to Joyce Ondersma, always the author's friend. Extraordinary thanks to Zondervan's editor-in-chief, Stan Gundry, for his support and encouragement when I needed it most.

1

Searching for Freedom

"I felt like I was put out to pasture, like an orphan, unwanted and unloved. No one but me knew the deep scars that I had inside. Even now, almost nine years later, I am still sensing great emotional scars that I thought were long gone."

These are the words of a woman who was rejected and abused, not by a boyfriend or a husband, but by a church. She still is not fully rid of the emotional and spiritual residue left from years of exposure to a church environment that was controlling, legalistic, guilt-inducing, and highly manipulative. "It's still hard for me to expose my wounds, to admit to other Christians that I have been hurt spiritually and that my emotions have been damaged. I thought I was able to put it all behind me, but I guess the memories will always be there."

Most people have been made aware by the news media of the tragic problems of child abuse and spouse abuse in our society. Physical and sexual abuse, unfortunately, are not new to the human scene. But until recently, very little attention was paid to what has become known as spiritual abuse. It takes place where we would ordinarily least expect to find something so harmful—in churches and religious organizations. We expect to be helped, not hurt, by pastors and others in positions of religious influence.

When our trust is violated by those who have been accorded society's respect because of their special role as spiritual caretakers and shepherds of God's flock, the pain, injury, and disillusionment can be devastating. Juanita and Dale Ryan state, "Spiritual abuse is a kind of abuse which damages the central core of who we are. It leaves us spiritually discouraged and emotionally cut off from the healing love of God."[1]

Spiritual abuse takes place when leaders to whom people look for guidance and spiritual nurture use their positions of authority to manipulate, control, and dominate. Or, as David Johnson and Jeff VanVonderen describe it, "Spiritual abuse is the mistreatment of a person who is in need of help, support or greater spiritual empowerment, with the result of weakening, undermining or decreasing that person's spiritual empowerment."[2]

Most people who are victims of spiritual abuse are sincerely seeking God, either out of a desire to serve him and know him more intimately or out of a deeply felt need to resolve problems. Being vulnerable in their spiritual journey, they would not knowingly subject themselves to pastoral or spiritual abuse. When they later realize that they have been involved in an unhealthy, abusive system, it is understandable that they may harbor resentment and bitterness against the leadership and against God himself. "Why did God allow this to happen to me when I was sincerely trying to know his will?" "How can I possibly forgive these people for the hurt and confusion they have caused me?" They may feel shame for having been deceived.

Do the abusers intend to inflict hurt? In most cases, probably not. They usually are unaware of what they are doing to people in the name of God. They may, in fact, be convinced that their behavior is what the Lord has mandated. What others interpret as control they may view as caring for the flock. Ken Blue notes that "spiritual abusers are curiously naive about the effects of their exploitation. They rarely intend to hurt their victims. They are usually so narcissistic or so focused on some great thing they are doing for God that they don't notice the wounds they are inflicting on their followers."[3]

What aspects of authoritarian churches are hurtful? What happens to members when they decide to leave or are dismissed? Are they likely to end up in another abusive situation, or are they able to find a "normal" church? What about those who find it impossible to return to church, any church? Is it possible to break the cycle of spiritual abuse? Can people find true freedom in Christ after years of bondage in performance-based lifestyles?

These are some of the questions we will address in the pages that follow. This is a book about the process of recovering from churches that abuse. You will be introduced to real people who have struggled with leaving dysfunctional churches and Christian organizations. Not all of their stories have a positive ending, but many of these people have discovered that it is possible to recover from spiritual abuse. We will try to identify the various paths toward recovery that the survivors of church abuse have found to be helpful. With a minimum of psychological jargon and considerable emphasis on case histories, we will explore the patterns of recovery that provide hope for healing and a context in which God's amazing grace can be experienced.

But first we need to describe the patterns of abuse, the factors that contribute to an unhealthy spiritual and emotional environment. We will begin with one young man's odyssey, a man we will call Carlos.

TRYING TO FIT IN

Carlos Garcia's story is typical of those of young adults who join what are sometimes called high-intensity or high-pressure Christian groups during their college years. Carlos became involved with an organization that is variously known as the Boston Movement, the Boston Church of Christ, or the International Churches of Christ (not to be confused with the mainline Churches of Christ denomination). *Time* magazine called this group "one of Protestantism's hottest churches," but in the same article critics called the movement "a real menace," "an authoritarian sect," and a "dictatorship."[4]

The movement is often associated with Boston because it was in the Boston area that the group was founded by Kip McKean in 1979. It spread rapidly through the United States, taking root primarily in metropolitan areas and recruiting many converts from university campuses. Wherever the church has expanded, controversy has followed. Carlos's story, though more extreme than some, illustrates why.

Carlos was born in Latin America into an upper-middle-class family and lived abroad in several countries before moving with his family to Los Angeles when he was fourteen. His multicultural background affected him a lot. He was fluent in several languages, but not English. To gain social acceptance he sought to excel in school. "I feel that I basically lost my adolescence because of the enormous cultural turmoil I was going through. I never really felt that I fit in anywhere."

After high school, Carlos enrolled at a West Coast university and lived away from home for the first time. He had a few friends—his roommates and a classmate or two—but still felt the emptiness of leaving his home and friends in Los Angeles.

As a pre-med major Carlos thought it would be good to learn something about Christianity in that most Western medical care systems are based on Judeo-Christian principles. His parents are atheists, so he brought no religious background to his university studies.

During the second quarter he was approached on campus by some young people from the Boston Movement. He accepted their invitation to attend a "Bible Talk." What impressed him most there was the sense of being "bombarded" by love, of receiving attention and acceptance given in Christ's name.

Eventually he felt pressured to attend more Bible Talks, and he went reluctantly, more because of the people he met than the theology he heard. Also, within the first week of his involvement with the group, they held one of their semiannual retreats at a downtown hotel. Looking back, Carlos said that the main purpose of the retreat was "to badger you into becoming a Christian." The retreat, featuring seminars conducted by key Church of Christ leaders, was directed mainly toward young adults and was an important part of the out-reach program.

Carlos recalls that seminar leaders "made fun of other churches and other so-called Christians, including those who had the fish symbol on their cars. But they made it clear to all of us that the real Christians were the people who belonged to their church, the Church of Christ. They are the real Church."

This elitist attitude is an example of what some call a "Christ plus something else" doctrine. That is, its advocates believe that faith in Christ is necessary for salvation, but the faith must be demonstrated within a particular church and in particular ways to be valid. Founder Kip McKean claims that he never taught that a person has to be a member of the Boston Church of Christ to be saved, but he admits, "I do not know of any other church, group, or movement that teaches and practices what we teach as Jesus taught."[5]

One "something else" for the Boston Movement is the view that water baptism is necessary for salvation and the forgiveness of sins. Within two weeks of that first encounter with the movement, Carlos was baptized. The acceptance he felt then overshadowed any misgivings he had about their teachings and theology.

Carlos stayed with the group for nearly a year. He was expected to be available to the church on what members called a "24/7" schedule: twenty-four hours a day, seven days a week. The daily regimen on weekdays included a prayer group at the start of the day and then, after college classes, recruiting teams to solicit new members, a Bible Talk, sometimes follow-up phone calls to prospective recruits, and a meeting with his "discipler." On Saturdays there was often a church-sponsored barbecue party, and on Sunday there were worship services. Studying had to be done late at night, and with the exhausting schedule, Carlos's grades slid steadily downward from the 4.0 grade point average he had achieved during the first quarter.

As a new member Carlos was assigned a "discipler," a person with whom he "fellowshiped" every day. Discipling—one-on-one instruction in the faith—is a common practice in many conventional churches, but the Boston Movement's approach has been criticized because the element of control is central to the relationship. Carlos soon discovered that his discipler sought to control the most personal aspects of his life. "They encouraged a kind of isolation from society," Carlos relates, "teaching that the world is corrupt and anyone criticizing the Church of Christ is speaking the words of Satan. We were told not to associate with those people." If the criticism came from family members, loyal followers were told not to associate with them either. When Carlos did go home for visits, he was asked to check in at least once a day with his discipler, who would always ask if Carlos had "shared" that day with family members and anyone else with whom he had contact.

Then Carlos was pressured to break his contract with the dormitory and move in with "the brethren," but his parents did not allow it.

Dating with "the sisters" was permitted in the form of a double date or group dating, but dating outside the church was strictly forbidden. Touching of any kind, including holding hands, was prohibited, and couples were encouraged to change dating partners every week. "If you really wanted to see a person again, you had to ask for approval from your discipler, who in turn would ask his discipler. If the person was new to the church, continued dating of that individual was discouraged. You were told that before you could have a serious relationship with another person, you had to have a good relationship with God. Marriage was encouraged only between 'seasoned' members of the church."

Carlos attempted to "share" with the few friends he did have outside the church, but they were skeptical and eventually lost interest in him. He felt alienated, but the response from the church members was, "See, this is how the world treats you. Now you can be with us until you die!"

In the meantime, the church was encouraging Carlos to become an evangelist because of his multicultural background. It would mean dropping out of the university. Carlos feels he was manipulated by a sense of guilt: "If you were asked to do something and you did not want to do it, you were told to 'Get out of yourself,' or that you were going to hell. You would be told that it was 'Satan telling you not to do it'; 'Christ didn't live a life like that and you must follow his pattern; if you are lukewarm, Christ will have nothing to do with you.' 'You're going to end up like the rest of the world.'"

Guilt was imputed in other ways also. Questions about the church or the Bible were tolerated, but answered with Scripture. If you questioned Scripture, you were made to feel very guilty. You were commended for being "fired up for God" and excited about the church, but if you demonstrated what were viewed as inappropriate emotions, more guilt was inflicted. Feelings of depression or sadness or doubt were discredited. Other members would ask Carlos, "What are you thinking right now?" and he got to the point that, no matter what he was really thinking or feeling, he should automatically answer, "Fired up for God!"

As Carlos became increasingly involved with the church, his mother realized that his personality was changing. She became anxious and eventually got in touch with someone who helped her understand that Carlos was involved with a cultlike church. She voiced her concerns to Carlos, but he would simply invite his parents to his church and remind them that they were going to hell. He never told his discipler about his parents' concern, but as his mother persisted, he began to have doubts about the group.

During the summer after his first year at college, Carlos was feeling depressed about his failing grades and asked the people at church what he should do. They replied, "If school is interfering with your relationship with God, then you should quit school." Carlos was not ready to do that, and this advice, he says, was the beginning of the end of his relationship with the church. When he told a staff member he wanted to leave the church, the leader replied, "You're free to go, but it's not God's will for your life." The leader brought up memories of friendships, the baptism, and other church events and started to cry when Carlos told him that he was determined to leave.

Carlos soon discovered that when you leave the Church of Christ, the members will not talk to you. He was shunned completely. His former non-Christian friends were not there for him either, so he had no one to turn to. He became very depressed and was unable to study or attend class. He received three warnings of academic dismissal, which he successfully appealed.

However, he began hanging around the pool hall to pass the time. This pattern of poor academic performance, depression, and loneliness lasted for three more quarters. Finally, late in his second year at the university he was expelled with a GPA of 0.74, but he could not bring himself to tell this to his parents.

The university allowed him to gain credits at a community college and then return to campus if he did well. He took six academic units and was living by himself in a condo. On the weekends he would go with some new friends to a pool hall in another nearby city. About three months later, he met some people who turned him on to crystal methamphetamine, which he used daily for the next six months. He was feeling very angry toward the Boston Movement. His experience had left him feeling embarrassed and bitter and, worst of all, isolated.

At this low period in his life, his parents paid him a surprise visit, but he still lacked the courage to tell them that he had been kicked out of school. Soon afterward, Carlos returned home and told his parents that he wanted help. He was considering suicide. His parents obtained counseling for him, and Carlos considered enrolling at another college.

Today at age twenty-one, however, Carlos is still a confused person with many unresolved emotional problems. He still feels angry toward the Church of Christ. He attends meetings of Alcoholics Anonymous, where his feelings are understood and he is accepted for who he is. He has nothing to do with church or religion.

FOLLOWING THE PATTERN

The case of Carlos Garcia demonstrates how an abusive, manipulative religious system can devastate lives.

Carlos was a young man passing from adolescence to adulthood without the familiar support system of home and family. His multicultural background had left him feeling uncomfortable and unsure of himself socially. The Church of Christ entered his life at the "right" time: he was vulnerable. The group surrounded him with an instant family of loving, accepting people. The church gave Carlos a focus, a sense of purpose, and an opportunity to avoid his anxieties and insecurities. Their theology meant little to him.

The evidence is compelling to those who have studied the phenomenon: involvement in a high-intensity Christian group can bring welcome relief from the pain and frustrations of everyday life. People in transition can be exploited and abused by spiritual leaders who turn out to be more like tyrants of the weak than shepherds of the sheep. In the book *Toxic Faith*, Stephen Arterburn and Jack Felton characterize the plight of people like Carlos:

> Persons with low self-worth feel alienated and isolated. They want to belong and be accepted. Toxic faith leaders know this. They can pick out wounded followers who are looking for someone to make them feel important. Under the guise of ministry they cater to people's weaknesses until those people believe they are receiving genuine caring. . . . Toxic faith practitioners find those with low self-worth and minimal boundaries. They ask them to trust just a little. With that first step of trust, the persons are flooded with affirmation and love.[6]

Like many other victims of spiritual abuse, Carlos feels embarrassment that he allowed himself to be "taken in" by the group. He wonders why he stayed as long as he did. Arterburn and Felton explain why: "The new followers don't turn astray, even when they see the exploitation, because they continue to reinforce their own decisions. They feel bad about themselves already, and admitting they had been duped into submission would be devastating. . . . If their self-worth had been present in the beginning, they would have discerned the unhealthiness of the group and refused to be part of it. . . . They don't see the exploitation because their low self-worth has allowed them to be exploited all their lives, so it seems almost normal."[7]

This pattern recurs frequently in my research. Its traits are recognizable in other case histories related in this book. Not all people who have low self-esteem or come from dysfunctional backgrounds end up like Carlos, but they are the most vulnerable to the wiles of abusive religious groups.

Another former member of the Boston Movement describes the plight of some who leave. "I know that when people finally decide on their own to leave, they are so beaten down and confused that they don't know what is true to hold on to versus what is false to discard. Many quit seeking God and give up on the church altogether."

Other high-intensity Christian groups besides the Boston Movement can be found on university campuses or in college towns. Parents of students involved in such groups often notice two characteristics: personality changes and a disruption of family relationships. One mother wrote to ask for more information about the Boston Movement: "I have a son involved with this church . . . and it has destroyed our family relationship." A letter from another mother was printed in a

Boston Church of Christ publication as part of a response to an earlier article about "detractors and depro-
grammers" who are critical of the movement. The
woman stated that her son changed after joining the
movement; he was no longer able to make rational decisions, concentrate very long on anything but the Bible,
or function without the continuing help of others in the
group.[8]

DISCERNING THE DIFFERENCE

How can we discern an unhealthy, abusive Christian
church or fellowship from one that is truly biblical,
healthy, and worthy of our involvement? LaVonne Neff
states that it is important to examine the effects that
groups have on the people who join them. "Good results
will not sanctify bad doctrine, but bad results can serve
as warning lights, *even where [the] teaching appears sound.
. . .* What happens to members' personalities, relationships, job commitments, community involvement? Is
the group's overall effect on those who come in contact
with it—members and nonmembers—positive or
negative? Is it an agency of healing, restoration and
reconciliation?"[9]

To distinguish between healthy and unhealthy
churches, Neff poses eleven questions.[10] Each question
points to conditions that make it difficult for people
like Carlos to put their lives back together upon leaving
an abusive church situation.

1. *Does a member's personality generally become stronger,
happier, more confident as a result of contact with the group?*

In an abusive church, the use of guilt, fear, and
intimidation to control members is likely to produce
members who have a low self-image, who feel beaten

down by legalism, who have been taught that asserting oneself is not spiritual. A leader in one group mentioned in this book used to tell members, "God never meant for you to be happy in this life." This is not to say that all members of authoritarian churches are unhappy, guilt-ridden people. However, one of the first disturbing characteristics to be reported by relatives and friends of members of these churches is a noticeable change in personality, usually in a negative direction.

2. *Do members of the group seek to strengthen their family commitments?*

Nearly all unhealthy churches attempt to minimize commitments to family, especially parents. Young people may be told that they now have a new "spiritual" family, complete with leaders who will "re-parent" them. Church loyalty is seen as paramount, and family commitments are discouraged or viewed as impediments to spiritual advancement.

3. *Does the group encourage independent thinking and the development of discernment skills?*

Control-oriented leaders attempt to dictate what members think, although the process is so spiritualized that members usually do not realize what is going on. A pastor or leader is viewed as God's mouthpiece, and in varying degrees a member's decision making and ability to think for oneself are swallowed up by the group. Pressure to conform and low tolerance for questioning make it difficult to be truly discerning.

4. *Does the group allow for individual differences of belief and behavior, particularly on issues of secondary importance?*

A legalistic emphasis on keeping rules and a focus on the need to stay within prescribed boundaries is always present in unhealthy spiritual environments. Lifestyle rigidity in such groups increases a member's guilt feelings and contributes to spiritual bondage. This rigidity is often coupled with an emphasis on beliefs that would not receive great attention in mainstream evangelicalism.

5. *Does the group encourage high moral standards both among members and between members and nonmembers?*

In intense, legalistic churches and religious organizations, the official, public proclamations usually place special value on high moral standards. In some instances, however, there is a double standard between those in leadership and those in the rank-and-file membership. For example, abusive churches tend to have incidents of sexual misconduct more often than most conventional churches; leaders sometimes exhibit an obsessive interest in sexuality. Unhealthy relationships and confused thinking often result for the members.

6. *Does the group's leadership invite dialogue, advice, and evaluation from outside its immediate circle?*

Authoritarian pastors are usually threatened by any expression of diverse opinions, whether from inside or outside the group. Displaying an attitude of spiritual superiority, they will reject any invitation to genuine dialogue and will often make a conscious effort to limit influence from outside the church. When outside speakers are given access to the pulpit, they are carefully selected to minimize any threat to the leadership's agenda. Coercive pastors are fiercely independent and do not function well in a structure of accountability. For the sake of public relations, they may boast that they are accountable to a board of some sort, when in actuality the board is composed of "yes-men" who do not question the leader's authority.

7. *Does the group allow for development in theological beliefs?*

Another hallmark of an authoritarian church is its intolerance of any belief system different from its own. I am not referring to clearly heretical teachings and doctrines that contradict the historic Christian faith as it is expressed, for example, in the Apostles' Creed. Indeed, abusive churches are usually very orthodox in their basic beliefs. The problem is that pastors in such groups are likely to denounce and discredit other Christians' beliefs and their expression of them. Authoritarian pastors tend to be spiritually ethnocentric—that is, they tend to measure and evaluate all forms of Christian spirituality according to their own carefully prescribed system, adopting an "us-versus-them" mentality.

8. *Are group members encouraged to ask hard questions of any kind?*

A cardinal rule of abusive systems is "Don't ask questions, don't make waves." A healthy pastor welcomes even tough questions. In an unhealthy church, disagreement with the pastor is considered disloyalty and is tantamount to disobeying God. People who repeatedly question the system are labeled rebellious, unteachable, or disharmonious to the body of Christ. Persistent questioners may face sanctions of some kind such as being publicly ridiculed, shunned, shamed, humiliated, or disfellowshiped.

9. *Do members appreciate truth wherever it is found, even if it is outside their group?*

Whether they admit it or not, abusive churches tend to view themselves as spiritually superior to other

Christian groups. This religious elitism allows little room for outside influences. There can be no compromise with external sources, who, the leadership will say, really don't understand what is going on in the ministry anyway. The only way to succeed in an abusive organization is to go along with the agenda, support the leadership, ignore or remove troublemakers, and scorn detractors and other outside critics who seek to "attack" the ministry.

10. *Is the group honest in dealing with nonmembers, especially as it tries to win them to the group?*

Sometimes abusive groups illustrate what I call "split-level religion." There is one level for public presentation and another for the inner circle of membership. The former is a carefully crafted public relations effort, the latter a reality level experienced only by the "true believers." Recruitment tactics are usually intense; even if they are not actually deceptive or fraudulent, they can be manipulative or exploitive. Sometimes high-pressure religious groups are evasive about their true identity: "We really don't have a name; we're just Christians." A healthy Christian group should have no qualms about revealing who it is and what its intentions are.

11. *Does the group foster relationships and connections with the larger society that are more than self-serving?*

Sometimes it is difficult to discern the motives of a pastor or church group upon the first encounter. As in all of life, first impressions are not always correct. Sustained contact with an unhealthy church, however, will usually reveal a pattern that is consistent with the characteristics we have identified. Members will be requested to serve, to become involved, to sign up for a variety of activities that, upon closer inspection, appear designed to maintain the system and serve the needs of the leadership. Abusive churches thrive on creative tactics that promote dependency. Emphasizing obedience and submission to leaders, these churches often require a level of service that is overwhelming to members, resulting in emotional turmoil and spiritual breakdowns. Instead of serving God and their neighbors, members are robbed of relationships with family and friends, which hinders rather than nurtures their emotional and spiritual development.

Carlos's experience in the Boston Movement impeded that development. The anxieties and insecurities that he sought to resolve were only intensified in the Church of Christ. Upon leaving the church, he found himself more depressed and isolated than ever. His life gives testimony that not everyone who leaves an unhealthy religious group will experience an adequate and wholesome recovery. All too many remain like Carlos—angry and confused people who bear the scars of spiritual and emotional damage and have not yet understood or experienced God's restorative grace.

2

Is There Light
at the End of the Tunnel?

"I woke up one morning and realized I had not thought my own thoughts for three years."

"One of the things that has been most distressing to me is to see the way the church can discard people the way you throw an old banana peel out the window, with no apparent care for them."

"The emotional adjustment of leaving has been really difficult for me. I think at times I was even suicidal because it's so drilled into your head that if you willingly put yourself outside of that church, you're obviously not in God's will anymore."

"It happened gradually. But after four years in the campus fellowship, I realized I had been stripped of my God-given individuality."

"There are so many heartbreaking things we have been through. Part of the difficulty is that we love those who led us down the destructive path. We now realize that for a long time we hated ourselves and found ourselves lacking in many ways, only to find out later that it wasn't us at all!"

"After leaving the movement, it has taken us two years to become semi-normal again, just *semi*-normal. It has been hard to associate with other believers, not to judge them. It's like a death in the family, like you've lost your best friend."

"I began asking a lot of questions, and then everything got worse. I was accused of having a pattern of slander and was given my three warnings. I was told I would be disciplined if I ever talked to anyone else about my questions. I was told over and over that I was in sin and that they feared for my life."

"We wonder, 'Why did God allow this?' But we also know that we never go through anything just for ourselves. When we come through it, we're equipped to help the next guy who is stumbling along, going through the same thing."

"I was thrown out of my church almost three weeks ago, excommunicated. I asked too many questions. I continue to pray for everybody who's still in the church, and I wish that I could talk with them. I wish they would come talk to me."

So speak former members of churches that abuse. They have experienced spiritual confusion, emotional pain, and relational disruption. Each is at a different place on the road to recovery. The churches that have contributed to their problems represent a broad spectrum of evangelical and fundamentalist traditions. Some are on the margins of mainline evangelicalism and would be considered quite extreme compared with conventional Christian church experience. However, many of the unhealthy churches I have encountered in my research are mainstream evangelical. I have received reports of spiritual abuse in congregations from many denominations, parachurch organizations, and organized ministries. I emphasize this fact, because we often want to believe that abuse happens only in radical churches far out on the fringe of religious society.

The people I have interviewed come from charismatic churches and noncharismatic churches, from large congregations in urban areas and small congregations in the countryside, from churches in the United States and churches in Canada. Unfortunately, spiritual abuse can probably be found almost anyplace in the world where there are large numbers of Christians. The church of Jesus Christ is, after all, composed of many segments, all subject to human frailty and temptation. And while there are many healthy churches to choose from, there are no perfect churches to emulate.

"THEY TOOK THE LIGHT AWAY"

Cecily Talbot grew up in a fundamentalist church in a small town not far from Philadelphia. The little church could best be described as very legalistic and controlling. Among the taboos were jewelry, makeup, and school dances. Of all the members of her family, Cecily suffered the most from spiritual and emotional abuse, especially during her high school years. Cecily is now married and trying to put her past to rest.

"One of the biggest effects on my marriage is that I tend to overreact in my relationships with my husband. If we are having an argument and he says something is my fault, it strikes a nerve in me, whether or not it is true. My church blamed me for things over which I had no control. I was outspoken and often challenged the leaders and their teachings. No one in the church was supposed to challenge anything, and questioning those in authority was especially frowned upon. We were all clones who followed 'the man of God' no matter what. I refused to do that because I wanted answers to my questions. Yet years of being in an environment of blame and accusation have taken a toll. So today, when my husband says that something is my fault or that I should have done something differently, it affects me and our marriage seriously."

Victims are always on the receiving end of blame. Because abusive church leaders typically blame members for anything that goes wrong, those who break free of the abuse either find it difficult to accept blame for anything or find themselves wallowing in self-blame. Madeleine Tobias comments, "Ex-members have a tendency to continue this practice of self-blame after they leave. . . . They may feel that there is something lacking in themselves, or they were not good enough for the group or the leader."[1]

For Cecily, sorting out the abusive system she had recently left and adjusting to the dynamics of marriage led to a crisis.

"When my husband and I had been married for about three months, we had a serious argument. I tried to take my life by swallowing an overdose of pills. In reality, it was a cry for help. What I was trying to say was, 'I need help. I need you to understand what I have gone through.'"

Cecily's experience with legalistic and performance-based Christianity had familiar results: a distorted self-identity, feelings of inferiority, and a sense of inadequacy. "My most vivid memories of that church are the yelling and the condemnation from the pulpit. Members were told that we were nothing and that we could never amount to anything. Now that I have left the church I know it is not true, but they destroyed my self-esteem nevertheless. . . . They took away what God gave us, the ability to take pride in what we had accomplished. . . . Everyone has something about yourself that you treasure and that you are proud of. They found the light that kept me going and took it away."

David Johnson and Jeff VanVonderen write, "People who have been spiritually abused tend to have a negative picture of self, or a shame-based identity. . . . Shame is an indictment on you as a person. . . . You feel shame even when you've done nothing wrong; you feel defective as a human being, and like a third-rate Christian undeserving of God's blessings and acceptance."[2]

Cecily also adopted self-destructive behavior. "I went to a Bible college in New England for one year. The church didn't want me to attend this college because they wanted me to be home where they could keep an eye on me. I was considered a rebellious teenager. All the other kids were given going away parties as they left for college, but when I left, I didn't get anything."

At college Cecily had a casual affair with another student and then had a string of relationships in which, as she puts it, "I used men as building blocks to make me callous to the hurts of the world and the self-esteem problem I had." She dropped out of college after one year, returned to her hometown, and found friends who drank and used drugs. She ran off to New York soon afterward, she said, "to get away from the church and everything I thought was holding me down and causing me to hate myself. I was looking for someone or something to guide me in my life. I didn't want direction from my parents and the church, but I knew I needed it in my life."

In New York she started a serious cocaine habit and became promiscuous. "I didn't know at the time why I was doing it. I snorted cocaine because I was around people who did and I wanted to fit in."

Cecily did not recognize then, as she does now, that the real problem underlying her behavior was largely the stifling, controlling atmosphere of the church that for years had put her down and regulated all aspects of her life. "No matter what the church tried to say about me, I wasn't basically a rebellious person. I believe I was a normal teenager who wanted to dress like other sixteen-year-olds and wear my hair and use makeup the way they did. I was not allowed to do those things. I was made to be something I wasn't.

"As hard as I tried, when I moved to New York, none of those values that were supposed to have been ingrained in me meant anything. There was a point at the Bible college when I felt extremely close to God, but when I went home, the church would have nothing to do with me. I was the black sheep. No one wanted anything to do with me except the people who drank and partied.

"Only in the last few months has my downward slide begun to change for the better. I have started to climb back up and am beginning to come to grips with what happened to me. I attribute most of my personal problems—my lack of self-respect and the abuse I inflict on myself—to that church. I don't know if I can recover. I don't know if there is a light at the end of the tunnel for me. It doesn't feel that way, and it doesn't look that way."

A CYCLE OF ABUSE

Cecily had found herself in a cycle of abuse. Like other forms of abusive behavior, emotional and spiritual abuse is sometimes perpetuated by being directed at other innocent people. "I was verbally abused by the pastor and his wife as well as by my parents. Because of that experience, I too have become an abuser, to myself and my husband."

Cecily has had recurring nightmares, some of them about leaders or other people in that church. Once she dreamed she was being burned and tortured by them. "I woke up because I literally felt the sensation of being burned. I woke up visibly shaken. It really alarmed my husband."

Research shows that it is not uncommon for victims of spiritual abuse to have disturbing dreams and nightmares. Reexperiencing trauma through painful memories or recurrent nightmares is one of the elements in diagnosing what has come to be known as "post-traumatic stress disorder."[3] This disorder should be treated through professional counseling.

Another effect of the abuse for Cecily was a lack of trust. "The church destroyed my family's unity and my ability to trust people. They pitted my sister and me against each other, but God has healed that bitterness and we are now friends. Every time I confided to some-body in that church, they turned against me or betrayed my confidences. My teenage concerns and problems became common knowledge to the whole congrega-tion. When someone breaks down a family's sense of unity and an individual's personal trust, they are des-troying two areas that are especially important to a teenager. That had major repercussions for me. Even today I have difficulty talking to people and believing in them."

Cecily is working to reestablish trust in others. Tobias comments, "The betrayal of trust by the group, with its residue of hurt, rage, and fear, presents problems for the ex-member. Knowing whom to trust and to what extent takes time. . . . The key to trusting is to proceed slowly. Trusting is a process, not a final act. It must be earned by those who desire to get close to you."[4]

By learning to trust again, the victims of abuse also discover that they can tolerate and trust themselves, an important part of the recovery experience.

KEEPING GOD IN THE PROCESS

Besides trusting people, victims like Cecily also need to learn to trust God again. Cecily struggles with the question of why God allowed her to experience all the pain. Is there a light at the end of the tunnel? "I keep ask-ing myself, why can't I recover from this? Why can't God take it away and make it disappear? If I could, I would let him. Maybe I am holding on to it as an excuse. I don't know. I'm very confused about why God would let me go through these things.

"I need answers. I need to find out where I go from here. If there is help, where do I find it? I know others have suffered much more than me. But my experiences have hurt me and affect me today. I sense the oppression of that church in my marriage. I don't know how to vent my feelings. I don't know how to look at my experiences and make something good come from them. My ways for crying for help, like taking overdoses and scaring my parents and husband, aren't working. I am anxious to find help and to talk to someone who can relate to my experiences.

"Sometimes I think about the day of judgment and standing before God. That terrible church will be accountable for what it did to me. I will be accountable for myself, for all that has happened to me since the day I stepped out of the church.

"I want to be spiritually, mentally, and emotionally stable. That church took away not only my self-esteem, but also my love for God. The only way I knew God in that church was from the screaming and yelling that went on in the pulpit. Yes, I turned away from God, but when I turned back toward him, he was still standing there, waiting. Now I need some guidance in my life and I want God to take residency in my heart again. I pray that I will find that help and that it won't be too late."

THE NEED FOR COUNSELING

Cecily's story is typical of victims who have not received some form of professional counseling. Whether that failure is owing to a lack of resources, a distrust of professionals, or uncertainty that help is really needed, this kind of person frequently is pessimistic about the prospects for full recovery. "The most frightening thing to me right now," said Cecily, "is the thought that I won't recover, that the actions of that church will affect me for the rest of my life. I don't know where to start or who to talk to. I have spoken with friends and ministers, but it seems that no one can help me. No one has ever said, 'I can help you. I've been there. I know.'

"Counseling takes time, and I have been hesitant about talking to anyone. But I know that I need help because it is affecting my marriage. The constant dreams are scary. I have to take pills before I go to sleep so that I don't dream, or at least so that I don't remember the dreams. It is horrible when you can't even sleep without these people creeping into your mind and thoughts. In my dreams I am always standing back looking at myself and seeing the people around me as uncaring and unaware of what is happening to me."

There is a sad irony in Cecily's cry for help in that she has not availed herself of professional counseling. That may be a result of the confusion and disorder that impede the process of resocialization into mainstream society. I believe that people like Cecily cannot make a full recovery strictly on their own. Some victims may find substantial help in talking with other former members of their church, attending special seminars, or reading books. The support of friends helps many through the ordeal; two friends helped Cecily kick her cocaine habit. But for some victims, these means alone are not enough.

Dr. Paul Martin, a Christian psychologist, believes that, although there may be obstacles such as a lack of finances standing in the way, a formal, systematic program of professional counseling is essential. A structured program enables victims of spiritual abuse to have a framework for dealing with their post-departure problems, thereby facilitating the recovery process.[5] However, Martin points out, it is important that the counselor not be a secular mental health professional having a bias against religious beliefs, who would discourage the victim from giving any regard to religion whatsoever.[6]

A Christian counselor is needed, whether a pastor or professional therapist. It must be someone who understands the dynamics of abusive systems and who, in a relationship of trust, can provide the warmth and caring necessary to support the victim. The survivor must be assured of God's unfailing grace and be able, in effect, to rediscover the gospel.

THE FALLOUT IN THE FAMILY

Cecily's family has been affected by the spiritual abuse as much as Cecily herself, especially in terms of the legalistic atmosphere. In *Breaking Free: Rescuing Families from the Clutches of Legalism,* David Miller states that legalism in a church renders dysfunctional everything a person touches, including family: "There is a corruption in the heart of the legalistic family that will eventually break through the surface and adversely affect the children. . . . The damage comes not from what is done to the children but rather through the more subtle messages they learn about themselves and others. . . . Legalism inevitably turns children into church mice and Christian leaders into authoritarian monsters."[7]

Cecily's family's only exposure to Christianity came in one church. For many years they accepted its performance-based teachings and incorporated them into their family life. Now her parents, who have since left the church, are torn with guilt for rearing their children in that traumatizing religious environment. Cecily's father says, "I'm glad that I left the church, but it was fifteen years too late. It is like being released from a prisoner of war camp. You get so accustomed to the guarded conditions that it is hard to understand what freedom is. You wouldn't go back, but it is difficult nevertheless."

Cecily's mother agrees. "You feel so glad to be out when you first leave. For all those years we weren't allowed to visit other churches, so it was great to be able to find other Christians, people who studied the Bible and who loved the Lord. We settled into a church fairly quickly after we got out. After the newness of being out wears off, you begin to feel the tremendous loss of the years that you were there. You don't feel that you really fit in anywhere."

The anxiety felt over "the lost years" is common to many former members of abusive churches or cults. Sometimes people go through a kind of grieving process as they reflect on "what might have been" if they had not been trapped in their situation for a long time.

Not being able to fit in is another common feeling of the victims of spiritual abuse. Studies reveal that when people experience what sociologists call "role exit," they frequently endure a period of anxiety and feeling in a vacuum. In one study of people who have left a wide array of social roles and become "exes" (ex-nun, ex-cult member, ex-doctor), sociologist Helen Ebaugh found that more than three-quarters went through a period of feeling anxious, at loose ends, and scared over not belonging or fitting in.

> The experience is best described as "the vacuum" in that people felt "in midair," "ungrounded," "neither here nor there," "nowhere." It is as though the individual takes one last glance backward to what he or she has been involved with in the past but knows is no longer viable. Yet the person isn't really sure at this point what the future holds. It seems that this last glance backward is necessary before actually taking the leap forward.[8]

Cecily's father observes that "we continually see the people who are involved in that other church. The leaders do not understand how badly they treated us. They think a simple 'I'm sorry' will make us feel better. They just don't get it. To this day, my family has nightmares about these people. We pray with the children at late-night hours because they have had nightmares about things that happened to them at that church.

"I enjoy visiting other churches and hearing the Word of God preached. But it is hard for me to read my Bible every day because of the regime I lived with for twenty years. I don't like to read the Bible. I don't feel a part of anything. I don't want to feel a part of anything.

"What would help me in recovery is to talk to someone who is farther along in recovery than I am. The honeymoon stage of being fresh out of the group, which for me was like being saved all over again, is over. I'm almost cynical.

"It is hard to be a part of anything anymore. I want to go to church and hear the Word of God preached, but I don't have any desire to become involved. How do you explain to other Christians the last twenty years? People try to be nice, but it is hard for them to understand."

The problem of not being understood is common among victims of spiritual abuse. Just about the time they find a "normal" Christian church and develop friendships and a trust relationship with the leadership, they tell their story to someone and in response are likely to encounter suspicion and skepticism about their spiritual stability, their mental health, or both. As a result, the victims feel guilty, misunderstood, and even rejected. They wonder whether they should ever again risk revealing their past.

Christians who want to be helpful to those who have come out of abusive experiences must be sensitive, non-judgmental, and accepting—even if they find it difficult to understand how something so bizarre could happen to another Christian.

MOVING FORWARD

In the meantime, both Cecily and her family are making progress, however slow, toward a wholesome recovery. Yet the process is not without regrets. Cecily's father states, "The greatest pain we suffer is over what has been done to our children. That is my hardest struggle." He adds hopefully, "We are seeking God. We ask his blessing and for him to direct us in what we do. We know he has taken us down a very rough path, but we believe that this experience will help us strengthen others. Maybe God can use us to help others recover, because we understand what they have been through."

Despite her uncertainty about the future, Cecily feels she is slowly moving forward. She is grateful for God's grace and for the married couple who helped her get off cocaine. Through her husband she has gained an appreciation of herself. "He came into my life at a point when God must have known that I needed someone to say, 'I love you. You don't have to sleep with men to be something; I love you for who you are.' My husband loves me for what I am, not what I can do for him."

Cecily, too, has regrets. "Now, I am a bit crass with people because that is my defense. I feel that my armor is to pay back all the hurts I have received. I would like for my shield to be God's love, but I have too much anger stored up inside me toward the church and my parents, and I don't know how to release the bitterness."

Such is the experience of one family who, having escaped an abusive church, are trying to rebuild their lives. The next chapter tells quite a different story about a woman whose family abandoned her early in life and who suffered through a succession of abusive churches before finally breaking free.

3

"I'd Like to Really Live, Not Just Survive"

It was a sad letter. "I love God, I hate people," she wrote. "Is there any hope for me? I think I will eventually take my life if I cannot find peace and Jesus."

Colleen Roberts (not her real name) had been tossed about in a series of church and personal relationships that had left her literally without hope. She had written to say that my book *Churches That Abuse* had helped her greatly. But it was clear from her letter that she was far from recovered from the spiritual, psychological, and physical abuse she briefly recounted.

Colleen had constructed a mental fence around herself and was not sure that anyone—counselor or pastor especially—would be able to penetrate that defense. "Nothing is allowed through my fortress anymore. There is a tiny mailbox on the outside of the thick castle wall. It holds 'help' for people like me, but I cannot reach it. I am a prisoner, alone and almost without faith. I am scared. I'd really like to die, but I know it's wrong to think that. I don't think I'll ever come around. I just pray for God to take me quickly, with the last bit of hope I have left."

The letter led to a series of events through which Colleen was able to reach into that little mailbox and begin her journey toward spiritual and personal wholeness.

Colleen's story will help us to understand two concomitants to spiritual abuse. First, like many members of abusive churches, Colleen had a personal history that predisposed her toward victimization. Second, her experience demonstrates the essential need for help from competent counseling and caring Christians in the process of recovery.

LOST AT HOME

Colleen's parents gave up custody of her when she was a teenager because they thought she was incorrigible. But she had watched many television shows about families and desperately wanted her and her parents and brothers and sister to stay together, to be, as she put it, "a real family."

"I wanted a mom and a dad who cared about me. My parents were very wealthy. My father was a businessman who traveled extensively, and my mother was rarely home. I took care of my little brother, who was ten years younger than me. I was the only one who ever got him out of the playpen. As children we were very isolated and lonely.

"My sister dealt with her pain by overeating and becoming very overweight. I was more vocal about wanting attention. I asked for my parents' attention in more ways than they could handle. I ran away from home a couple of times and stayed with friends whom I felt cared about me.

"The first time my parents tried to give up custody, the judge refused, and they were quite angry at having to take me back. They locked me in my room on my birthday. I snuck out; they took me back to court, and I was put in a group home."

Her parents' rejection drove Colleen to attempt suicide at age sixteen, after which she was placed in a private mental hospital in Baltimore. After three months she climbed a ten-foot-high, barbed-wire fence, dyed her hair, and hitchhiked to see some Christian friends in Connecticut.

"Even though I didn't understand much about Christianity, these people seemed different to me. Because they seemed to care about me, I felt I would be safe with them. They let me stay with them for a few days, but were unable to keep me because they were trying to adopt children of their own and I was a runaway. They did what they could for me by sending me to a Christian group home for troubled teens called His Mansion."

His Mansion is an independent organization run by Stan Farmer, a man who, according to Colleen, has no formal training or official connection with any established church. "Stan arranged for me to stay at the Mansion until I was twenty-one, at which time the State of Maryland would allow me to leave. Stan became a father figure to me, and I called him 'Dad.'"

Colleen's first impressions of His Mansion in 1973 were favorable. She was able to complete high school and enjoyed structure and attention, a loving "father," and a group that told her how much they cared about her. It seemed that this was what she had been looking for. But Colleen soon learned that appearances were deceiving.

"Stan had been in the military, and he treated us as if we were in the army. One time the only meat in the house was a turtle that someone had caught. I slept and ate very little. I used to stay up until midnight doing laundry. They made us do it over if we didn't do it right. We had to cook and clean up after about twenty people. Then we had to do homework and the Mansion's required Christian studies. We were often exhausted. I remember hiding in a closet hoping they would think I was sick and leave me alone.

"There were seven or eight girls and the same number of boys living at His Mansion. It was one big home, but the girls and guys lived on opposite sides of the house. We were never allowed to have much contact with the opposite sex. Most of us came from needy families. We didn't have strong father figures in our backgrounds, and Stan loved playing the role of father. If we were told that we needed a spanking, we knew that it was for our own good."

Colleen says that Stan began to have sex with her when she was eighteen, after she had graduated from high school. "His Mansion was my first encounter with Christians, and I was very trusting and desperate to be loved. When I went to live in Stan's home with his wife and children, something seemed strange, but I wasn't too worried because they claimed to be Christians. Stan would come up to my bedroom in the mornings to wake me up. It seemed odd, but nothing happened at first. I didn't have a model of what a father should be, and I wanted a father. I thought that was what fathers did. I was very naive.

"The main philosophy at His Mansion was to obey authority at all times. I obeyed everything, including having sex with my 'dad' and running away when I got pregnant. There definitely was a form of mind control at His Mansion. Stan was the central figure, and we all did exactly as he said. In addition to Stan, there were two female counselors on the staff. Looking back, I don't think that the counseling I received there was very professional. My interaction with the counselors was very limited. Stan made all the important decisions. I didn't think anything of it; I thought that it was because my 'dad' loved me.

"I came from a dysfunctional family into a Christian family that taught me about Christ, authority, and sex. I had been raped twice at age fifteen, and all I knew was that I had been forced by two strangers and now I was having sex with Stan, my 'father.' He had taken the place of my father who had rejected me completely and I loved Stan as a parent. I replaced my own unhappy family with Stan and his family. I was so thrilled to have a family of my own.

"Stan continued to have sex with me at least twice a week for two and a half years. When I became pregnant with his child, he manipulated things to look as if I ran away. The rest of the group didn't know that he was the father. I looked like the bad daughter who had backslid and would always be that way.

"Stan had found an apartment for me and my daughter near His Mansion. Since he would not admit to being the father of my child, I had to go on welfare. He had a key to my apartment. I remember waking up in the morning and his fondling me even though our daughter was in the same room. I felt I had no other choice because this was my dad. If I got rid of him, I was afraid that I would have nobody.

"When I turned twenty-one, I received papers from the State of Maryland saying that I was free to go. For the first time in my life, chains had fallen off me. I knew no one could come after me and get me if I ran away. I could do whatever I wanted to do."

Colleen had no employable skills because the Mansion taught girls little except domestic tasks and Bible studies. She had been totally dependent on the group. Left destitute with no one to turn to, an elder in the church Colleen was attending at that time suggested that she try to work things out with her parents and perhaps return to them.

STRIVING TO BE GOOD ENOUGH

When she finally contacted and met with her parents again, her father would not acknowledge Colleen or her daughter, but her mother admitted that she felt guilty. Her sister, who was in Silver Spring, Maryland, invited Colleen to move there to join her in a Christian group that I will call "the Community."

"I moved back to Maryland and joined the Community, whose name has changed several times. The group was not communal in the strictest sense of that word, although most members live in the same neighborhood.

"For the first two months I was there, I was told to call my elder every day. I was a single mom, which put me in the lowest level of the community. Single moms needed to be watched because we weren't 'spiritual.' I soon learned what heavy-handed shepherding was all about. For example, when I joined the Community, I was told that if I wanted to know what God was saying, I was to go to my discipling elder and ask him. If a member wanted a job, he had to go to the elder who would pray about it and then tell you what God wanted you to do.

"When we joined, we gave our allegiance to the Community, not to God. I remember saying, 'I pledge that I will obey my elder, no matter what.' Everyone clapped when I said that. I never said anything about being loyal to God. We even signed a covenant."

Friendships outside the Community were forbidden, even with high school friends who lived nearby and wanted contact with Colleen. There were forms of isolation inside the Community as well. "The elders told me to spy on the people in my household. I was not allowed to eat or fellowship with them, but I was supposed to spy on them. The more I spied on them, the higher I rose in the elders' opinion. In return for betraying my friends, I ate like a king at the elders' houses. I was praised continually and I felt very loved."

Colleen eventually moved into the home of one of the home group leaders, who converted the basement to an apartment for Colleen and her young daughter. This was a common arrangement for single mothers in the group, who were then put to work in the elders' homes.

When working for the elders, their cleaning "duties" as well as their lives were closely scrutinized. "Everything we did in the Community had to be thorough." A preoccupation with thoroughness is common in abusive systems—what Stephen Arterburn and Jack Felton call the "tyranny of perfectionism." These writers comment that victims of spiritual abuse, because they are taught that they are part of a special church, "believe they can attain perfection, believe they need to attain it, and feel terrible shame when they do not attain it. They all strive for perfection and make themselves sick in the process."[1]

Colleen found that being obsessed with faithful performance brought, not joy, but feelings of humiliation and inadequacy. "I remember washing their marble floor with a toothbrush, sweat pouring over my headband into my face and then seeing the elders come in wearing their three-piece suits. It was humiliating, yet they told me that it was good for me to humble myself."

She continued to experience guilt manipulation and performance-based Christianity. "I was told that I would never be good enough. Now, years later, I have learned that the Law says I will never be good enough, but God's grace is sufficient and God really loves me. There is no difference between an elder and me. I am not worse because I am a single mom. I am not a second-class Christian, which is how I was treated in the group. I felt like a pig, sweating on my knees, preparing for the elders who were coming in for a meeting and a luncheon. I was supposed to regard it all as a privilege; it was a privilege to work in the elders' homes and to be that close to them."

Some people fall prey to spiritual abuse because they have compliant personalities and do not realize soon enough how they are exploited. People like Colleen, write Arterburn and Felton, "cause no problems because they believe everything that is passed down from the top. . . . They never make a fuss and never rock the boat. They just wait to carry out the next duty that is assigned. . . . Everyone acts as if it is a great privilege to be taken for granted and lost in such a worthwhile mission."[2]

In addition to controlling weaker members with unreasonable demands, the Community leadership arranged and supervised dating relationships. "They had me set up with one man whom I never liked. I loved the Lord and wanted to know more about him, and so I wanted a relationship with someone who wanted the Lord as much as I did. Instead they deliberately put me with 'John' because he wasn't very interested in the Lord. I was a single mom and therefore could not be considered spiritual. I went to the elders several times about John because I didn't love him and the relationship wasn't working out."

It was five years before she was allowed to date another man they had chosen.

While living in the home group leader's home, however, Colleen found once again that her single-mother status and her need for love made her vulnerable. The home group leader began to harass her both physically and sexually. One time Colleen's sister saw some bruises and became concerned. Colleen relates, "I didn't tell her because she was the one who had brought me into the Community. I told her that I was mugged in the parking lot." Nevertheless, her sister reported her suspicions to the elders. That, Colleen said, "was the beginning of the end."

The elders did not believe Colleen's sister, and Colleen found herself subjected to many forms of harassment in daily activities.

GRACELESS RELIGION

Being a creative person gifted at flower arranging, Colleen was eventually allowed by the leaders to take a job at a floral shop even though it was standard policy for single mothers to receive welfare and work in the elders' homes. She held down a full-time job and took care of her daughter, but she was still expected to watch the home group leader's children and do half of the housekeeping. Colleen increasingly despaired of meeting the expectations of the group. "I was exhausted. There was no way I could do everything they wanted. I became worse and worse in the elders' eyes. I was a rebellious backslider.

"My discipling elder and I had a pretty good relationship until that time, but he started saying things like, 'I'm going to have to let you go if things don't change. You'll have to get another person to sponsor you if you want to stay here.'"

At that point, one of Colleen's friends who had left the group earlier stopped by to see her at the floral shop. "I showed her the bruises, and she was horrified. She started seeing me every day at lunch and told me about her church. She was going to the National Presbyterian Church because she wanted something as far removed from the Community as she could get. She insisted, 'You have to talk to somebody. You can't keep getting beat up like that.' I eventually agreed to get counseling from someone at National Presbyterian Church."

She was not in counseling for long, but long enough for the elders to become suspicious of Colleen's activities. Her elder told her she would have to leave. For the second time Colleen had experienced graceless religion. "The Community never preached the grace of God. I could never be good enough. That was their key to controlling me. I felt like I was being whipped the entire time I was with them. I was the kind of person who could easily be controlled. I would have done anything they said. 'Obey' was the key word at both His Mansion and at the Community."

Like others, Colleen discovered that it is folly to dissent and point out flaws in an abusive system. An abusive church exists in a world of denial, and all steps must be taken to ensure that the good name and image of the group are maintained. There can be no admission that there might be chinks in the armor. Arterburn and Felton comment, "Anyone who rebels against the system must be personally attacked so people will think the problem is the person, not the system. . . . Anyone who hints at not following the rules is dealt with quickly so the organization . . . will not be damaged."[3]

Colleen did tell the elders about the physical abuse, and one appeared to believe her but later on turned against her. At that point she decided to leave the group. "I was upset that this elder could use as an excuse to change his mind the fact that I was a single mother and then tell me that I was loose, had no morals, and had probably encouraged the home group leader to come on to me. I could not win, so I left the group."

Colleen remembers her last encounter with the home group leader who had harassed her. "I had one box of glass momentos left in his house and was told to pick it up when the leader and his wife were not at home. It turned out that he was home when I came by, and I watched him drop the box down the stairs. Everything in the box shattered."

THE TEMPLE AND BEYOND

"I went to the parents of some of my non-Christian friends, saying that I was afraid I was going to die because I was out from under the spiritual protection of the Community. They let me stay at their house for about two weeks. They called the police to arrange for police protection because my old boyfriend had bothered me. Finally, the woman who had encouraged me to get counseling at the National Presbyterian Church and another ex-member took me and my daughter into their household. They had set up a home for people like me who had left the Community and had no place else to go.

"The man I eventually married, Bill, had also been a member of the Community. In fact, he was considered to be elder material. We liked each other while we were there, but we were not allowed to date. One time, when I was working in the flower shop, I brought him a plant and had to sneak it to him when nobody in our household was home. That was the beginning of our relationship, although we were never allowed to date or see each other.

"Sometime after I had left the Community, he, too, had to leave because he had gotten a girl pregnant and was no longer considered elder material. He was crushed because all this time he had been groomed to be an elder, and now he was being treated like dirt. He found me at the house of my two friends. We became like two scared chickens, holding on as tight as we could to each other. He was on drugs at the time, and I was an emotional mess.

"Bill and I found another church called the Temple [a fictionalized name], which turned out to be very much like the Community except that they met in an actual church building. We naively thought that having a building meant that they were different enough from the Community so that we could feel safe. But they had the same kind of structure, the same kind of rules. It was a nondenominational church. They didn't live communally, but we were encouraged to live in households if we could. I had my own place, but it was right across the street from the church. They kept in touch with me all the time. I had counseling once a week with a woman who was a very powerful elder in the church.

"Bill and I were married in the Temple, but we didn't stay there very long. Bill's parents wanted us to leave because they could see how much control the church had over us. Our marriage was already in trouble. Bill was abusive to me. When I was pregnant with our son, I almost miscarried. Bill was the child of alcoholic parents, and I was very immature. We clung to each other. We thought we were Christians, but despite years and years of being in Christian groups, neither of us knew Christ at all. Neither of us knew how to depend on Christ. When we were in the Community, other people had told us what God was saying, but now we had nobody."

Colleen and Bill eventually divorced. Once again she had to try to pick up the pieces of her life and start over. "The Temple found out that I had left Bill. They invited me back and set me up in an apartment near the church. I was also placed in counseling with the same woman elder who had worked with me before. I became very close to her and almost loved her like a mother. I was still very needy. I loved her despite the fact that she told me what to do all the time."

When she rejoined the Temple, Colleen continued to be controlled and rejected. "I was being humiliated again. I was divorced, and divorced people were discouraged from dating and never really forgiven.

"When my ex-husband came back into my life and wanted to spend more time with me and our little boy, I felt that, according to the Bible, I should try again to make my marriage work. The Temple said definitely not; I could not remarry him. They encouraged the divorce, but when I was divorced, I became a nobody."

The leaders at the Temple used various forms of spiritual intimidation to add to Colleen's confusion. "One day, when I was supposed to be at a meeting, I wasn't feeling well, so I sent a note explaining that I was ill and would like to be excused from the meeting. The counselor referred me to Pastor John. He and the woman counselor talked to me, and she asked, 'Do you want a spanking from Pastor John?' He said, 'I will spank you if that's what you're looking for.' He was really going to spank me. I couldn't believe it! I was embarrassed.

"The Temple taught that if you did not speak in tongues, you probably had sin in your life. They believed in what is called 'slaying in the Spirit.' If your eyes rolled while you were slain in the Spirit, you had an evil spirit. They always emphasized the activity of demons. I supposedly had lots of demons, and they prayed over me many times because I was being rebellious. I was being stubborn because I wouldn't let it out, but I didn't know what I was supposed to let out."

Eventually Colleen moved to California to be near her mother. "My parents are divorced. I wanted grandparents for my kids because they had no one. The Temple was still in contact with me in California. At that point I was almost suicidal. I had been in abusive churches all my life. I didn't know if I could ever find a safe church. I had been controlled all my life and now I was on my own in another part of the country with no money. I was a mess."

Despite a brief, long-distance encounter with the Temple, Colleen's recovery began after she returned to California. An initial step was to contact some friends from her days at His Mansion. She was determined to set the story straight about her daughter's father. "I had to speak up," Colleen said. "I had kept quiet too long." Stan tried unsuccessfully to intimidate her into silence.

Stan has acknowledged his paternity and his sin and has contributed to the financial support of his and Colleen's daughter. His Mansion, which Stan Farmer still directs, remains a highly structured program. Living conditions have improved considerably over the last decade at least with respect to better food and counselor training. The rehabilitation program has had a beneficial impact on the lives of hundreds of young people.

LEARNING ABOUT GRACE

What made Colleen aware of her psychological and emotional needs as a victim of spiritual abuse? Through the recommendation and financial aid of Christian friends, she entered the Wellspring Retreat and Resource Center, a professional and residential community near Columbus, Ohio. Wellspring is devoted to helping persons who have come out of what staff member Larry Pile calls "TACOs"—"totalist aberrant Christian organizations." The director is Dr. Paul R. Martin, a Christian psychologist, who along with others on the staff was once a member of an abusive church.

"For the first time in my life," Colleen relates, "I heard about the grace of God. And for the first time I understood what it meant that Christ died for my sins two thousand years ago. While in those bad churches, I kept thinking that I was getting more wicked all the time. I loved God so much, yet I believed that he thought I was dirt. Everything depended on how much my abusers loved me. If they were mad at me, God was mad at me too. I really believed that.

"The most important thing for me was realizing that God loves me. I always accepted what the elders told me, which was that you had to earn love. I thought God responded in the same way. God picked Cain and Abel; one he liked and one he didn't. I was the one he didn't like. Now I realize that isn't how it is."

Some victims of spiritual abuse are reluctant to pursue professional counseling because they are wary of allowing another authority figure into their lives. Colleen was apprehensive as she entered Wellspring because she did not really know what was in store.

"When I was picked up at the airport, I thought, 'Here we go again. I'm just in another group situation where they will tell me more of the same stuff: what to do and what to believe.' It took me a few days to get used to it, to feel safe. I remember asking Dr. Martin, 'Do you even care about me?' He said, 'I care.' And I could tell that he really did. I wasn't just another ex-member; I wasn't a number. He was not just repeating things he had told a hundred other people before me. By the end of the week, he knew me and my life."[4]

She had begun the journey to recovery.

According to Martin, the people he sees at Wellspring usually go through three stages of recovery after leaving a cult or authoritarian church.[5]

THE FIRST STAGE

The first stage of recovery involves "exit counseling" and confronting denial. Victims will tend to deny their experiences and blame themselves for what happened to them. They need to be shown that they were controlled by very clever, manipulative people.

Learning to trust others in authority without creating a new codependent relationship is one of the first issues that victims of spiritual abuse confront. They need to understand how the control mechanisms that were at work in the church continue to affect them even after they have left. They must experience true acceptance, love, and a sense of belonging. They need to understand what has happened to them emotionally and psychologically.

It is important to help victims experience positive fellowship. The intensity of relationships within an abusive group must be matched by intense relationships in a wholesome setting.

The first stage also must address the doctrines of the abusive church. It is important to examine and carefully refute any unorthodox teachings. Most of the churches mentioned in this book are theologically orthodox, although nearly all would be guilty of distorting the Bible's message in some way. Peter Sommer observes, "These groups are rarely heretical in theory.

They don't deny Christian basics; they tend to brush by them. Instead they focus on what makes them different from other churches or groups. They have lots of teaching, but it tends to be on such themes as commitment, submission, and prophecy."[6]

Stephen Martin, a staff member at Wellspring, considers instruction in sound study methods and the interpretation of the Bible important. In abusive groups, twisted hermeneutics are often used to instill fear and guilt and thus become a form of spiritual intimidation. "Since leaders of abusive churches typically twist the Scriptures, education in hermeneutics would help the ex-member gain the right perspective on Scripture passages. In talking with former members at Wellspring, I have found a number of them who have difficulty with or even an aversion to reading the Bible because it has been misused by the group to abuse them. Learning the proper application and interpretation of Scripture goes a long way toward healing the wounds of abuse."[7]

Sommer advises, "It may be wise not to read Scriptures that the group has emphasized; their interpretation may be deeply grooved into your thinking. Read instead the many texts that they did not teach you."[8] I suggest that these people attempt to rediscover God's Word through the Psalms because those writings validate a person's individual spiritual life. Paul Martin feels it is wise for victims to use a different translation of the Bible from that commonly used in the group.

THE SECOND STAGE

The second stage of recovery from Wellspring's perspective is both a time of grieving and a time for regaining a sense of purpose. Tears will be shed over wasted years, missed opportunities, and severed friendships. It helps to talk about the past. Colleen comments, "Talking to others about what has happened to me has really helped me." Former members need a safe place to tell their story fully and freely, even if they feel confused and embarrassed.

The abusive church experience is often a crisis of faith, as Paul Martin and others have pointed out. Victims must be able not only to rebuild self-esteem and purpose in life, but also renew a personal relationship with God. That can be difficult for those who have yet to resolve the tough question, "Why did God allow this to happen to me when I was sincerely seeking him?" As Rachel, one former church member, puts it, "I had been taught that nothing was ever God's fault. The problem was that I was a true, believing Christian, but when I asked God for spiritual bread and water, look what I got. Was I praying to the wrong God? Was I dishonest? Secretly evil? Was I demonic, like the church kept telling me I was? How could an honest, sincere believer get tricked like this? How could God let this happen?"

People like Colleen and Rachel need the assurance that it is possible to have a rich relationship with God. In Sommer's words, the victim must be turned "to faith in the living God from faith in a distorted image of him. Your break with the group is a step of obedience to the first commandment: No graven images!"[9]

THE THIRD STAGE

For Wellspring, victims of spiritual abuse have reached the third stage of recovery when they begin to talk less about the past and begin to focus on the future: career pursuits, new relationships, and family. It is a time for picking up the pieces that are worth retrieving from life as it was before the abusive church experience.

Paul Martin describes his experience of retrieval this way: "Without question, parts of me died during those years in this group. I have been able to take the discipline that I learned in the group into my current career. But I constantly try to recover the parts of me that died during that involvement."[10]

One woman tells of her having been forced to discard all her prized record albums of a certain kind of music upon joining the Jesus People USA. During her recovery she searched second-hand shops so she could replace those lost albums. The third stage also means coping with resocialization and the practical matters which it entails such as managing time and money, relating to public agencies and institutions, learning parenting and other special skills, and adjusting to making decisions for oneself. Establishing credit, preparing a job résumé, and even opening a bank account may be new experiences.

Wellspring exists because recovering emotionally, restoring a loving relationship with God, and re-entering society are not easily accomplished on one's own. The accounts in this book reveal how tortuous the path to recovery can be without professional, caring help. The tragedy is that for the victims of spiritual abuse, the options are disappointingly few. Not many programs are especially equipped, as Wellspring is, to treat victims of spiritual abuse. Moreover, the costs can be out of reach for people upon leaving a control-oriented group because they have few financial resources. It is also the case that beyond the sphere of Christian counseling, some psychologists and psychiatrists are biased against all religious beliefs and may encourage clients to rid themselves of all religious entanglements, proverbially throwing the baby out with the bathwater.

But for many victims, like Colleen, counseling offers renewed hope.

TO LIVE, NOT MERELY SURVIVE

As Colleen continues to sort out the experiences of more than twenty years in abusive situations, she is beginning to understand more clearly the ugly dimensions of her victimization and why she cannot trust other people. Tragically, like other victims of abuse, she sometimes feels that she deserved the abuse, that she was a bad person, that she didn't measure up, that she could never make it on her own in life. She made this very insightful observation: "As much as people like me are not acknowledged as important in abusive groups, we are the ones who build them up. I have given them much energy and power because I can be controlled so easily. They love to control people like me, but in reality they think we are dirt. It all adds up to a very exploitative relationship."

In the book *Toxic Faith*, Arterburn and Felton reinforce Colleen's observation:

> Victims make great sacrifices. . . . They unknowingly sacrifice their needs so that persons they esteem can be saved from experiencing the consequences of their own behaviors. Although they are unaware of it, their attitude of sacrifice has more to do with a lack of self-worth than anything else. In the name of God,

they sacrifice far beyond what God would demand. The ways in which they give of their time, money, and themselves perpetrate the exploitation by a ministry that is not dedicated to serving God. The more the victims sacrifice, the more victims are created by the ministry.[11]

Colleen's moving from one abusive situation to another points out a dilemma of victims. More than half of the people I interviewed in the research for this book come from dysfunctional families. They endured abuse, lacked love and attention, and had very low self-esteem.

Colleen has learned that she fits the profile of a passive-submissive-dependent person. "These kinds of people," she explains, "begin with a clinging neediness and a search for acceptance. They deny their own strengths and see those whom they are dependent on as stronger persons. They readily submit to abuse and look up to authority figures. They feel empty. They don't absorb well. They limit their world. They look for the good in suffering situations. The churches that I have been in look for that type of person.

"The other people in the groups I joined were just like me," Colleen says. "I thought my sister was a much stronger person than I, but when I remember how she ate her problems away, I recognize that every one of these traits fits her too. It makes me ill to think that a strong person could actually be on the lookout for someone like me and say, 'We know she thinks she's dirt, and that is what we'll feed on.' To do that kind of thing consciously is the worst kind of abuse."

In view of all that Colleen has experienced, it would not be surprising if she had concluded that God is a "victimizing" God. Others who have been repeatedly disappointed by a shabby, exploitive substitute for biblical Christianity have discarded the faith altogether. That is not the case with Colleen. She confesses, "Through all of this, I really love the Lord. I know he is real. He has protected me so many times; I am a survivor. But I'd like to know how to really live, not just survive."

4

"Grace to People Who Know They Need It"

It is customary for authors to include dedicatory statements at the beginning of their books. One such statement caught my attention because it relates to the subject of this book.

> To everyone to whom the words of a pastor have become wounds to the soul

This is the dedication statement chosen by Ron and Vicki Burks for their book *Damaged Disciples*.[1]

The wounding words of a pastor are all too real for a Christian couple whom we shall call Miriam and John Bower. Their story is somewhat different from others told in this book, because the Bowers were an affluent couple who moved easily in society when they began attending the Marin Christian Life Church in Northern California.

73

Miriam had been one of the "flower children" in the drug and hippie subculture of the sixties. Years later, she met John while they were both in a Twelve-Step program to recover from substance abuse, and they married three months after they met. While in the program they also became attracted to Eastern religions and the New Age movement.

IN SEARCH OF A SPIRITUAL FOUNDATION

"We were very disciplined in our New Age search for truth," Miriam relates. "We had an altar in our home where we meditated each morning and a guru whom we followed and whose picture was next to Jesus' on the altar. The New Age movement is a spiritual smorgasbord, and we were involved in many aspects of it. We attended an Episcopal church, but had no idea what Christianity was all about. We had a fish symbol on our car and idols in our home. We subscribed to the basic beliefs of the New Age: We are gods, and we create our own reality. We began a very successful business. I had two children from a previous marriage, and together we had three more children.

"We had difficulty making our marriage work because *I* thought I was God and my husband thought *he* was God. We were converted at a Christian marriage conference associated with Campus Crusade after we were presented with the Four Spiritual Laws. We asked Jesus into our hearts and came home from the conference different people. We didn't really know what had happened to us, but with the guidance of the Holy Spirit, our lives began to change. We had never been around Christian people or exposed to biblical Christianity. We started reading the Bible and realized that we had been born again. We threw out our extensive New Age library and destroyed our meditation table and idols.

"We found a very biblical church, which we attended for two years. There were many solid Christians there who came from Christian backgrounds and had grown up with family devotions. It was wonderful for us. With five children, we wanted to learn to be Christian parents. We were learning Bible stories along with our children.

"After a while we became rather critical of the church. We didn't understand why they didn't take stronger positions on some issues or why they allowed some people in the congregation to smoke or drink rather than telling them what they should and shouldn't do.

"At that point, we visited an Assemblies of God church called Marin Christian Life Church. We were swept off our feet on our first Sunday there. The pastor yelled, ranted, and raved. We loved the whole emotional experience. After the service, people came up to us and said, 'The pastor doesn't usually come across so strong.' We told them that it was wonderful. In retrospect, I can see that what appealed to us was the haughtiness and arrogance we sensed. There was a spirit permeating the church that said, 'We are better Christians than anybody else. We are the only true Christians in Marin County.' John and I really liked that.

"Because of our affluence, we were immediately given special status when we joined and had access to the pastor and his inner circle. In that church, wealthy members were courted while needy ones were ignored. Our susceptibility to flattery and position unfortunately caused us to overlook the warning signals of trouble ahead.

"We had been strongly family-oriented, but were told that this was wrong. We were advised that we should not have any more children, that we should attend every church service—we were expected to waken and pack our five children into our car to sleep in the parking lot while we attended the daily 5:30 A.M. prayer meetings—that we should not home-school our children but put them into the church school, and finally, that we should move closer to the church because we were too isolated."

The Bowers began to see other signs of a controlling environment. "Symptoms of dysfunctional families abound in this church. There is denial and cover-up. Members desiring to discuss or work through problems are publicly labeled as the source of all problems in the church. Many members come from abusive backgrounds and are already accustomed to victim status. Feelings of shame, humiliation, inadequacy, and dread are systematically drilled into the members from the pulpit because no one measures up."

Conflicts arose between John and Miriam after a few months, in part over how much they should be involved in the church work. "I was never completely submitted to the church, but my husband was," Miriam says. "I had always been an independent person and was not the type to submit to anything.

"Our marriage had been shaky from the start, but we felt that Jesus had healed it. In this new church our relationship became dysfunctional again. Eventually they put us into counseling. At the first session we had to sign a release allowing the counselor to discuss our sessions with the pastor and his wife. We knew from experience that this meant we would become subject matter for the pastor's sermons and his wife's gossip.

"We left the church after two years. We had many issues to deal with. We lived a half-mile from the church on a dead-end street, so every time we went anywhere we had to pass by the church. We had to take our children out of the church school because they were told that their parents were 'listening to Satan.' The pastor called on us repeatedly, because he did not want us to leave; we had made a commitment to the building program."

After leaving the Marin church, the Bowers found a small church of fifty members that helped them to rebuild their faith and come to grips with the shortcomings of their former congregation. "The pastor was very loving, kind, and caring," Miriam said. "I felt that God led us there because that was where we needed to be to begin a healing process. I heard the Scriptures with new ears. It was almost like a second conversion experience. I began to see that in that unhealthy church, my relationship with God, which was extremely close after I had been born again, had been interrupted. I didn't have that direct connection with God anymore. Someone had come between God and me and interfered with God's direction for my life.

"The pastor preached plainly on the Scriptures and talked about Jesus' words concerning love, hypocrisy, and judgment. Many Scriptures came alive for me again. The one thing that was really missing in Marin Christian Life Church was love. Instead there was judgment. In this new church it was like coming out of a terrible accident or illness because we had to break through webs of misinformation that had been getting in the way of our relationship with God."

TAKING RESPONSIBILITY

"Another issue we had to confront was our being left with nothing. The church had stripped away all our relationships with our family and friends and anyone who wasn't in the church. We knew many people who had left the church before we did. One of the first things I did was to call them and apologize because, like everyone else, I had stopped speaking to them.

"We became close with some of these former members. At first we all talked about how we felt the church should and would be brought to judgment. However, eventually I realized that I had to stop pointing the finger and thinking about what people had done to me and start asking myself some very real questions about what I was doing in this new church. To me, that was the real turning point in my recovery. Our recovery—the understanding, forgiveness, and healing that were necessary—took about a year. It took some of our friends two years to be healed and to forgive, and others still longer.

"I thought about starting a formal support group. I felt that the Twelve-Step program I had gone through earlier had helped my recovery from the abusive church. I had instinctively gone through the twelve steps without realizing it: I admitted that I was powerless over this abusive group; I asked God to help me; I did a thorough inventory of my faults; I made amends and apologized to people I had hurt and reestablished relationships I had cut off; I sought to strengthen my relationship with God.[2]

"The main thing was that I had gone beyond being a victim and pointing the finger and blaming the people who had abused me. I started looking at myself and asking what God could teach me from this situation.

"When I analyzed why I was at the Marin Christian Life Church, I realized that my character was much like the pastor's. We are more the oppressor than the victim. I was there because of a tremendous need to feel superior to anyone else. That appealed to me about that church: the 'us versus them' mentality. We were supposed to be on the cutting edge of Christianity. Then I started to see the judgmentalism and the pride in my heart. Many of the Scriptures that I had not been able to comprehend or make real in my own life—such as 'the beam in your own eye'—became very clear.

"I realized then that God had actually done a wonderful thing to take us through that experience. I don't want to have those non-Christlike attitudes. God was able to cleanse me of that. I have became a more loving, less judgmental person. I am a very different person from what I was before I went through that experience. Looking back, I can honestly say I am really glad I went through it because it revolutionized my Christian life. I like me better the way I am now."

John also found that he had to take a hard look at himself. "I became aware of what a fool I had been. My spiritual pride was revealed to me. The Marin church supplied some of the negative needs in my own character and helped to bring them to the surface. I think God used that to expose my real flaws so that my character could become more like his.

"I was a real Nazi type of person while a member of this church. Consequently, I had to face some ugly truths about myself when we left. The main thing was that I had to start using the mind God gave me rather than be governed by my emotions. My initial response when I left was anger. My initial response was that I wanted to expose them to the media. God quickly squelched that idea. We would have done damage to the Body of Christ if we had followed through. We realized that we had to let God deal with them.

"Then we realized that we were talking as victims and finally had to look at the part that we played in it. Nobody forced us to go there. We had walked in with our wits about us and had participated fully and voluntarily. So we had to look at what it was in ourselves that made us want to participate. For myself, I had to see my spiritual pride, that part of me that wanted to be a super Christian, to be on the cutting edge of Christianity.

"I was and still am a person with a mental outlook that sees everything as black or white—no ambiguity. The absolutes we found in that church fit very well with who I am. We could put people into boxes, situations into boxes, and that enabled me not to think. It is a very lazy way to go through life. But I have found out that things aren't always black or white. Discerning what God's will is in each given situation isn't always easy.

"I came to realize that I had to take responsibility for this kind of thinking and its consequences. Take responsibility, confess, and don't blame the church or the leadership. Of course, it was quite a blow to realize that I was responsible for all that I had done to my family. I had brought them into the unhealthy spiritual environment. I had to repent and tell my wife and family that I was sorry."

MAKING A COMPLETE BREAK

On the basis of their experience, John Bower advises people who are contemplating leaving an abusive situation to make a complete break and flee. They themselves did not. They kept their children in the church school for a while, but John says, "That had a devastating effect on them." A daughter remained in the youth group, but she soon left by her own choice.

John's advice is noteworthy, because many of the people I have interviewed have been undecided whether to leave or to stay in the hope that their presence might make a difference. They feel that by abandoning the situation, they will also be deserting friends who need their support and who might also be persuaded to leave. I believe it is naive to think that they can effect change in an abusive situation. David Johnson and Jeff VanVonderen observe,

> If . . . there is a bottleneck of power-posturing leaders at the top, who are performance-oriented, the chances of things changing are very slim. . . . Sheep follow shepherds. And those who do not leave will tend to become entrenched in domination and legalism, whatever form those take.[3]

Furthermore, by remaining in an unhealthy environment for whatever reason, people help to perpetuate a system they have experienced as destructive.

> By staying and contributing your time, money and energy, are you helping something continue when, honestly in your heart, you disagree with it? We believe that if everyone who was doing this would stop, many very unhealthy and abusive organizations would be unable to continue functioning.[4]

Making a clean break externally, however, still leaves a process for becoming free internally—that is, spiritually and emotionally. Johnson and VanVonderen have identified four things that need to happen in order for people to become truly free.

First, victims have to reach the point where they realize they are being spiritually abused, and ask for help. They must be given the information and permission necessary to call what they've experienced "abuse."

Second, they need a renewal of the mind. In a very real sense they've been spiritually brainwashed. They must be immersed in the truth about who God really is and what He has lovingly done to settle the issue of their value and acceptance. They need to hear the good news about their new *gift-based* identity.

Third, they must experience safe relationships in which to heal from their emotional, psychological and spiritual wounds. Admitting neediness is hard. Looking at yourself honestly and fearlessly is hard. Much support is needed.

Fourth—again, in the context of safe relationships—they must be given permission and opportunities to practice getting their sense of identity as a gift from Jesus.[5]

The Bowers' experience of escape and recovery generally parallels these four stages.

In time the Bowers returned to the first church they had attended as Christians. "The people there welcomed our return, saying that they had missed us," Miriam relates. "They had no concept of what we had been through and couldn't seem to understand it. Most members of healthy churches, fortunately, are never exposed to something like that.

"A wonderful aspect of going back there, too, was that whereas I had been judging them before and thinking that they were not strong enough Christians, I realized now that they had a unique ministry. They were Christlike in their approach. They do a lot of outreach ministry with people who are divorced. Rather than being judgmental and asking for a conversion on the spot, they allow God to work on people individually. That makes sense to me because of how God worked in me. He helped me dispose of those things from my past that needed to be thrown out. God is powerful enough to speak to each of us individually without someone bossing us around."

John reports, "After we had been gone from the Marin church for about a year, we sent a short letter to the pastor and his wife saying that we forgave them for the hurt that we had suffered there. It was a way to cut them loose in our minds. It helped my recovery to go through this symbolic act. I felt a real release afterward. That forgiveness isn't something you can pretend to have. You have to go through the process and really mean it, really feeling it."

John's final comment serves as a summary of the basic message of this book: "The healing process cannot be rushed. It takes time, and each person's experience will be different. But through it all, God's grace is more than sufficient. He loves to give grace to people who know they need it."

"THE PAST DOES NOT HAVE TO RULE THE FUTURE"

Another couple who struggled in their marriage during their recovery are Bryan and Cyndi Hupperts.

They are former members of an organization variously known as the Potter's House, the Door, and Christian Fellowship Ministries, founded by Wayman Mitchell.

Bryan, who now has a career as a musician, tells his story first:

"The first thing you have to do when you come out of any abusive situation is to take responsibility for what you did. I knowingly walked into the situation. Yes, there was some deception. I didn't know there was a hidden agenda. Yes, they preached Jesus and the gospel. But they also preached that if you left their fellowship, you 'might stay saved, but you forever lose your destiny in Christ.' That amounts to spiritual intimidation.

"We didn't know how to function outside the group. It was like coming out of prison after thirty years. Basically, we had to start over. Day by day we had to put one foot in front of the other and say, 'Jesus, I have been a disciple of my denomination. I have been a disciple of my church. I have been a disciple of my pastor. I want to be your disciple and follow you.'

"In the organization we were associated with, they would twist the words of St. Paul: 'If you want to follow Jesus, follow me.' Anyone should understand that passage to mean, 'This is what a Christian life is. Look at what I am doing; this is how you follow Jesus.' But this is not how they meant it. That unhealthy church became the central focus of my life. My relationship with Jesus was relegated to a place of unimportance.

"But anyone who comes between you and your relationship with the Father is wrong. There is one mediator between us and God, and that is Christ. I had to learn how to walk with God, to hear his voice for myself, and to read his Word for myself, not just accept what the pastor said. The Scripture says, 'Work out your own salvation with fear and trembling,' and when I took responsibility for my walk with God, it was a scary thing. Now I am enjoying it.

"One morning I felt the presence of the Lord in my home very strongly. A verse of Scripture came to me: 'Restore to me the joy of my salvation.' He did that. Now I really enjoy the Lord and the fellowship of his saints. The church we came out of called other Christians 'religious devils,' but I discovered that there are other real Christians out there.

"I had problems relating to pastors for a time after we left. We hopped from church to church because most of the people didn't have a clue as to what we were going through. Sometimes I didn't want to tell what had happened to us because people didn't understand. One pastor said that I reminded him of someone who had gotten divorced.

"The key to any healing process is forgiveness. It starts with that. The word 'salvation' means to be made whole, and that is what God does. The Scripture says God gives beauty for ashes. Is there anything more worthless than an ash? But God will give us beauty for that, and it all starts with forgiveness. Forgive yourself and the people who hurt you. You may even want to forgive God. I was angry with God, even furious with him. I said, 'I love you. I serve you. How could you let this happen to me?'

"Then I remembered the biblical story of Joseph and the notion of how God was working out an eternal purpose in his life. Joseph told his brothers at one point that what they intended for evil, God turned into good.

Perhaps there was simply no other road for Joseph to take but the one that took him through the prisons and false accusations. In the same way, I believe that when Paul says, 'This light affliction, which is but for a moment, works within us an exceedingly great eternal reward,' it means that God allows us to go through these times with the ultimate purpose of conforming us to the image of Jesus. If something horrible happens, either you can respond in bitterness or you can say, 'Yes, Lord, use this to make me like your Son. Bring out more of his character in me. Let me decrease and let him increase in me.' That is true healing.

"I had my heart broken ten thousand ways. But there comes a time when you have to accept the past as the past. The past does not have to rule the future. Leave it behind. Set your eyes on Jesus and walk with God. Now I can say, 'Thank you, Lord.'

LEARNING TO TRUST AGAIN

"Another healing element has been my baby son. Seeing how trusting he is, I have been able to see God as a loving Father and have begun to trust other people again. I had to make a deliberate decision to trust. I am not going to look at everything with a jaded eye, but I am not going to be foolish, either. I was taken advantage of once, but I made up my mind that, yes, I am going to attend another church and, yes, I am going to trust its pastor as a man of God and hold him accountable to the Word of God.

"I know many people who have left Potter's House whose lives have not been healed. They have become bitter and cynical. But I choose to trust and to walk in love and the Spirit. I have chosen to experience the peace that Jesus' death and resurrection purchased for me.

"One more thing restored to me is compassion. I am not witnessing to someone just to bring another soul into the kingdom. That is a real person there. I am convinced that the reason most evangelism doesn't take hold in the hearts of the hearers is that we have based it on receiving instead of giving. We go out expecting to get a convert instead of sharing and ministering out of concern and compassion and letting Jesus minister his love through us. In the fellowship, everything was work and evangelism. The message was, 'Get out there and bring them in.' In reality, it meant, 'Get out there and bring the tithers in.'

"When we left the fellowship, my wife and I were terribly afraid. We had virtually cut ourselves off from family and friends. We had no place to turn. I came close to having a nervous breakdown. We were afraid, day and night, that 'they' might come after us. With some other organizations we knew about, there had been some physical violence against former members. That's not typical of this organization, yet we were afraid because we were so alone.

"I wanted to reestablish relationships with people I had treated rudely when I was in the group. I had to go to them in humility and repentance and say, 'I'm sorry.' Jesus said, 'By this will they know you are my disciples, that you have love for one another.' People have told me that I have changed. They say, 'You're alive, not a blank-eyed zombie walking around spouting Scripture.'"

Cyndi recounts having feelings and experiences that paralleled Bryan's in many respects.

"When we first left the group, God was very good to me. My frustration and hurt was vented all in one night when a couple of very good sisters from another church who knew me well took an evening to pray with me. After a long session of tears, God gave me the strength to forgive the abusers and to chalk everything up to experience. As simplistic as it sounds, this was no easy matter. It took obedience and a trust in my God like I never had before. It may feel good at first to take vengeance for yourself instead of leaving it up to God, but since we are not capable of judging righteously, our vengeance will not bring about God's will.

"It helped when I came to understand that nothing is in vain, that God has a purpose in everything. Through it all, God always gave me the strength I needed, so I knew he was going to use my past. We were able to minister to a lot of people who left authoritarian churches. If not for our own experiences of anger and betrayal, I don't think we would have been effective in that role. And the experiences of my traumatic childhood enabled me to help some troubled teens."

"WE LEARNED HOW TO LAUGH TOGETHER"

Bryan and Cyndi struggled to keep their marriage together after they left the Potter's House. Again Bryan cited the crucial need to regain trust.

"When my ability to trust was restored, it helped our marriage more than anything. Our marriage was strained after we left the group, and we didn't know how to communicate with one another or how to act like a real married couple. We were supposed to be one flesh, but we didn't know each other outside of the context of the group. I have a great wife, and I have come to appreciate and love her. We have forgiven one another, and God has healed our relationship.

"A practical thing in our recovery was that we began to go out and do things together. We started dating again. We did things like going to a park or a movie. We learned how to laugh together. That helped us. But I am by nature a rather insular person."

Bryan's private nature was a big obstacle for Cyndi to overcome.

"Coping with my husband when he was going through immense turmoil was a battle I was not equipped to handle. I could not understand why it was so easy for me to put the past behind me while it was not easy for him. Also, while still undergoing 'detox,' as I call it, my husband was still trying to flex his 'I am headship, wife; submit' muscles. It was frustrating. We had many battles, and it was all because we had forgotten how to respect each other while we were in that church.

"The hidden battles in Bryan's head gradually became evident to me. His self-image had been destroyed, and he began to withdraw from me. I could see his face awash with anger, and he would clench his fist in frustration, and I knew he was thinking about his past again. In those moments, the smallest issue would be blown out of proportion. He would misunderstand my intentions, and I, lacking patience and understanding, would react in anger and fuel the fire. Even the smallest effort by anyone to bring direction to our lives, if it wasn't presented to Bryan in gentleness, was misunderstood as a personal attack against him. He was distrustful of advice and very wary of anyone in authority.

"The idea had been ingrained in him was that he would never amount to anything if he ever left the Potter's House. My husband was paralyzed with fear many times because of this lie. When we moved to St. Louis in an attempt to leave the past behind, he had a little trouble finding good employment at first. This only reinforced what he had been told. Daily I had to keep building him up and encouraging him that he was a skilled person, that God would help him find a good job, that God would make him a good provider for his family.

("Let me say a word about God's provision. We never once did without during those tough times. One hot summer day I was recovering from the flu and wanted some orange juice. I was disappointed that we couldn't afford any. We were walking down Grand Avenue in St. Louis in the middle of the afternoon, and there was no one else in sight. A can of frozen orange juice came rolling down the sidewalk. It still had frost on the sides! We looked to see who it could belong to, but we couldn't find anyone. My husband turned at me and said, 'Honey, I think it's for you.')

"Because most of Bryan's battles were in his head, I felt frustrated, knowing he was in turmoil and not being able to help him. Then the book *This Present Darkness* by Frank Peretti came out. Reading it gave me a better understanding of what we were faced with. My prayer for my husband during those times was that he would put on all the weapons of our warfare, particularly the helmet of salvation and the shield of faith, so as to stand firm against the lies that were permeating his mind.

"I have learned that everyone heals differently, and it is wrong for me to expect my husband to heal the way I did. In the same way that everyone responds differently to God's invitation, our healing processes were unique to accommodate our different personalities. We had won one war by leaving the church, but there were times when we came close to losing our marriage because of the effects of all the indoctrination on our lives."

"We had to learn that our marriage was sacred and that we really did love each other. It took us a year of intense struggle, but I finally realized that our marriage is important to me and I would do whatever it took to save it. That is a decision I will never regret."

Cyndi reflects on the recovery process in these terms:

"From this experience, I have noticed a common factor in everyone who recovered and continues to serve God. They had a relationship with Jesus prior to joining such an organization, or they cultivated one while in the organization despite the propaganda fed to them. Sadly, I know quite a few people who left the church who are not serving God today, and I think it's because they really don't know who God is. They only know what they were taught and have a distorted image of God.

"Bryan and I have come a long way since we left the Potter's House. We have been greatly blessed. Our marriage is strong, and we have really grown to love and respect one another. God has blessed us with a beautiful son. Our finances are better than they have ever been. We own our own home and we are happy.

"For anyone who has left an abusive church and feels like they're sinking, I would encourage them to find Jesus. Look to him and cling to him the way the people of Israel looked to the brass serpent when they were plagued with snakes. Jesus is the only person who can help you battle all those hidden enemies in your head. Remember that it is Jesus who is the author and finisher of your faith, not the church. You get your sense of worth from Jesus, not the church. It is possible to leave an authoritarian church and still serve God."

5

"Next Christmas, We'll Get a Tree"

Eric Wilson spent nearly twenty years with the Assembly, a network of Christian fellowships with headquarters in Fullerton, California. Melodie was there eighteen years; Elizabeth Walsh, fourteen. They all mourn lost years and what might have been.

The Assembly congregations, founded by George Geftakys, are located primarily in university towns because student ministry has been a major focus of their work. Eric and other former members' experiences in the Assembly have a familiar ring: hierarchical leadership, an authoritarian style, a demand for unquestioning loyalty, control over family life and marriage relationships, rigorous discipline, and an often frenetic schedule of meetings, Bible studies, and church work.

Eric was initially drawn to the group through Bible studies and the participatory style of the worship services. He quit college, joined the Assembly, and eventually helped to start a brothers' house, where single men could live together—and where a rigorous set of rules governed their lives.

93

"When we started the house, the members were told to write down what we thought the purpose of the house was. The other brothers wrote things like: to learn discipline, to be more Christlike, to receive help with various behavior problems. I wrote down as my objective: to learn more about the Lord and to grow in grace."

After Eric married, his wife joined him as a leader in the brothers' house, and they continued to live there after they had children. Eric worked at whatever jobs he could find that did not interfere with the Assembly schedule. If schedule conflicts arose, he was counseled to find another job. Then, as their children approached adolescence, Eric and his wife felt they should seek a job transfer, move out of the brothers' house, and live on their own. Eric informed the leaders of their plans, but also said they did not want to leave the Assembly. The leaders would have none of it.

"The brothers told me I could no longer lead the prayer meeting that I had led for many years. Then they told me I would have to step down as 'leading brother.' Next, they told me that I couldn't preach on Sunday afternoons since I was no longer a leading brother. During Sunday morning meetings three brothers would usually speak. The last speaker was the main one and summarized and commented on the two previous speakers. Now they would not let me speak last. At that point I had not said a critical or negative word about the group. However, I felt that they had made some bad decisions and were not doing what was right.

"On my last Sunday I was the second speaker. I talked about knowing the will of God individually, based on the gospel of John, where Jesus tells Peter to follow him and Peter says, 'What shall this man do?'

The Lord said, 'Don't worry about that. Follow me.' I talked about the need for us as individuals to follow the Lord Jesus Christ. There was nothing in my talk that could be considered divisive. I didn't mention anything that would contradict any doctrine taught by the Assembly.

"The last brother followed me and preached on unity and standing together. He said Satan misleads us and tries to get us as individuals to go out on our own. Afterward, people came up and said, 'They were saying you were of the devil. What's going on?' I made excuses for the other brothers. I was protecting them to the very end."

"THE GOSPEL IS NOT ABOUT A LIFESTYLE"

The turning point came soon afterward. Eric was eating lunch in a restaurant and preparing a Bible study for the Assembly. "An old man started to tell me about his own troubles, a story filled with sorrow and pain. I was impatient because I felt I didn't have time to listen to him. He had bad health, his wife had just died, and just before she died, she had joined the Jehovah's Witnesses and had wanted nothing more to do with him. His daughter was a transsexual. He looked at me and said, 'I don't know why I'm telling you this. I never talk to complete strangers.'

"I don't know if the man even heard what I said to him, but God used the occasion to speak to me. This man was in pain and needed me, and I realized that the gospel of Jesus Christ was meant to meet the needs of people like this guy. The gospel is not about a lifestyle that requires being faithful to a system or a group. God got my attention that day and showed me that he cares more about individuals than a system.

"That night I spoke about that experience to the group, and afterward a brother asked me, 'Do you really think it is more important to talk to people in restaurants than it is to be prepared for the meetings? What values are you communicating to the saints here when you say something like that?' I had no answer for him. In my heart I knew, however, that something was wrong. They weren't preaching biblical Christianity.

"When I left the Assembly, I was very confused. I felt numb. I felt as if I had made a very big mistake. For twenty years I had set aside my concerns because I felt that Brother George's teaching was truly God's message from the Throne and therefore my concerns were, no doubt, of the flesh or of the enemy. After all, if you are being given 'God's message' from 'God's servant' who has 'God's anointing' for 'God's work' concerning 'God's testimony,' how can you really question it?

"It has only been since leaving the Assembly that the fog of deception and the fear have lifted and we have begun to see what we were involved in and how emotionally and spiritually damaging it has been. But the road to recovery has not been easy. For example, my wife and I found it hard to enjoy ourselves because we would remember all the activities that we used to be involved in almost every night. We felt guilty because we were staying at home when we should have been out doing something. It was as if a load was lifted from me, yet I wanted some of it back. I didn't know where I was without the parameters that the group provided. I had enjoyed the feeling that I was needed by people in the group. It was hard to realize that they didn't really want or need me. I still love them very much. I'd like to restore a loving relationship with them, but I won't do it at the expense of the truth.

"The most important thing in my recovery has been the need to get the proper balance between the heart and the head. In the Christian life, the mind is not something to be subjected to the heart. It is false to say you cannot know or understand the Word of God unless you have the proper inner attitude, or unless you surrender and submit, and that only when you get to that place will God break through and show you the way. Instead, the gospel is clear and easy to understand. It is not a puzzle that we have to put together. We place our faith in what the gospel teaches, then the emotions will follow, and we can have the proper emotional balance in our lives.

"We have benefited greatly from the writing and scholarship of many evangelical writers who speak clearly about the grace of God. A friend gave me commentaries and other books about Scripture to read so that I could find out on my own what the Bible really says. I still believed much of what George taught, but I had to set my emotions aside for a while. I couldn't devotionally read the Bible any more because I kept hearing George's blaring voice saying that I was evil, out of the will of God, and not going the way of the Cross. As I began to read and to understand what Christianity is really about, I was able to control my emotions."

THE COST OF SPIRITUAL CONFUSION

"My wife is still angry," Eric relates. "She doesn't understand why God led us into this group in the first place. She feels cornered, and she's not going to give up that independent spirit that they were always trying to get out of her. In her heart she knew they were wrong. She wants to see justice done.

"They hurt her as well as me. The Assembly shunned her. The acceptance she wanted from them was withdrawn. She would say hello to a brother and sister, and they ignored her. After twenty years of service, my family and I were treated heartlessly. We were rejected, viewed with suspicion, shunned, and humiliated."

Alienated and abandoned, they search for a church where they can feel at home, but it proves elusive.

"We have been to four different churches in the two years since we came out. I liked the first church we went to, but my wife and daughter didn't like the 'worldliness' of the congregation's lifestyle. They were different from what we were always told the committed Christian should act and look like. My family wasn't comfortable there.

"I had a chance to talk to the pastor of the second church we visited. This pastor emphasized commitment, but that was all I had heard for the last twenty years. I think Christians need to hear about the nature of God and his grace. The pastor said that his people knew that already, but it was something I hadn't heard much preaching on.

"We finally settled into a little independent Baptist church. A few months ago the pastor and an elder paid us a surprise visit. My first thought was that we had done something wrong, but because I had given the pastor a copy of the letter I had written to the Assembly, he thought we had been in a cult and weren't saved. That has strained our relationship.

"I have come to the conclusion that we will never get what we need from a church. It is going to be our family and the Lord, and we have to get that relationship right. There is not going to be a church suited for people who have our background. They won't change their ministry to meet our needs."

The Wilsons' youngest daughter is trying to adjust to the changes by blending in with her peers and being a bit rebellious, arguing and complaining.

"Our eldest daughter feels more comfortable in a strict environment. She doesn't want a TV and would probably like to go back to the Assembly. She knows, however, that the Assembly is wrong. She would probably fit in better in another conservative group that has a more legalistic orientation. She has come back from youth group meetings in tears because the other kids are not being serious about the youth pastor's message.

"My daughters are being home-schooled because my wife is fearful of their getting involved in public schools. And we're still nervous about the youth group.

"We are so thankful that the Lord has brought us out of the Assembly. It takes time to heal; it is difficult to face having to begin all over again. We feel depressed sometimes, yet not hopeless. We once again have a full salvation and all the joy that goes with it, as God intended."

MAKING EVERYTHING A SPIRITUAL ISSUE

Melodie spent fourteen of her eighteen years in the Assembly in a sisters' house, which, like the brothers' house, was governed by strict rules. Among the problems she encountered in the Assembly are spiritual intimidation, blaming the victim, and hypocrisy.

Melodie recalls being served something for dinner that she really disliked and that everyone else knew she disliked. She was told that she had to be willing to do whatever God wanted. "They spiritualized everything. My problem was not being humble before God, but I demonstrated humility in eating something I hated. This happened frequently. Once I was irritated at some minor thing and my roommate told me I couldn't leave until I had the joy of the Lord. We argued, and it became a spiritual issue. Finally I just said, 'Okay, I have the joy of the Lord now,' and left. They give little things eternal significance.

"Problems are swept under the rug. You are told to take everything to the Cross and identify yourself with Christ. What would Christ do in this situation? Would he cry, get angry? If you had been abused or raped, you were told that it was all in the past and that the Cross was taking care of it. As a result, people did not experience true emotional healing. They say the Lord will meet all your needs, but they cut off the means that the Lord has given us to meet those needs. They have a very narrow and distorted view of who God is and what he requires. You don't complain to the Lord's people.

"They always put the problem on the person. If you are upset at being told to do something unreasonable, you are being stubborn. Christ would do it, why won't you? The leaders would tell you that there is no reason for you not to do something unreasonable. You must be willing to be nothing and go the way of the Cross. If you are having problems with something, you are looking at yourself and should look to the Lord. That approach can be guilt-producing.

"They teach that if you are disobedient, you can forfeit your eternal 'inheritance' and miss out on the kingdom. You feel that you must always be doing more to please the Lord and, therefore, you are afraid of what will happen if you fail. When you leave, you lose your friends, but you wonder if you have lost the Lord too.

"Leaving was very difficult. All ties with friends who remain in the Assembly are severed—by them. My best friend returned a gift I had sent her. We know she has been counseled not to have contact with me. We are the enemy and when we contact members, it is a demonic act. They hope that defectors will feel the pain of rejection, repent, and return. I can't remember anyone leaving with their blessings. If you leave, it is because of some sin in your life."

FULL OF ACTIVITY, BUT EMPTY INSIDE

Elizabeth Walsh was another member of the Assembly who was eventually compelled to say no. Attracted to an Assembly congregation in Chicago while in her late teens, she was initially impressed with its emphasis on commitment and its desire to "be like the early church." After a time she moved out of her parents' home and into the sisters' house; she quit college because of the rigorous schedule of meetings and work set for her. Eventually she discovered that the wrong rules and too many rules can lead a person away from God rather than to him.

The Assembly limited Elizabeth's relationships. When she joined the group, she was told to give up her friends on the outside. She struggled to gain acceptance and friendship, but even after ten years she still felt alone in the crowd.

"Even though my life was full with activity, I was empty inside. People told me that if I worked for God, God would give me that perfect husband I was waiting for. Nobody cared or noticed me. I realized that I had developed emotional problems. I would laugh for no reason at all. I was giddy. I was unable to interact with people in a normal social manner. I felt like I was waiting for reality to come. I was in a temporary purgatory that I had to go through until I got to whatever my real life was going to be.

"As time went on, I got bitter. I got especially bitter about the roles of the 'workers.' Workers were considered holier and better than the rest. If George acknowledged you as a worker, you were at the top. Before you reached that pinnacle, you advertised your good deeds so that they would be remembered, and this news of your great spirituality would get back to George and then he would make you a worker.

"Over time, I began to get another view of the workers. I discovered that they were not better than the rest of us, they were not the holy people that folks said they were. They treated others horribly. They lacked kindness and compassion. In the Assembly, we never learned how to be kind.

"The biggest problem was my weight. The Assembly labeled me a glutton. Every meeting they would check my weight. 'How come you haven't lost the weight yet? God hates gluttons, sister.' Because I wanted to be married, they told me I lusted too much after men. I wanted to be a wife and mother, and I knew I wasn't 'lustful.'

"At the age of twenty-four, I finally made friends with two black people who joined the Assembly. I was told that there was something wrong with me because I had 'lowered myself' to have black friends. None of the white women wanted to be my friend. Black members never knew what the rest of the group thought about them."

ON FORGIVING AND FORGETTING

Elizabeth asked to be transferred to the Assembly in Champaign, Illinois, but she found that the labels and criticisms followed her there from Chicago. "Nothing was ever forgiven and forgotten. A small indiscretion would haunt you forever and be blown out of proportion.

"At age thirty I was asked to live in my own apartment because I had a reputation for asking questions. It was the first time I had lived on my own without others looking at everything I did. I didn't know what to do with that kind of freedom. Nobody made any effort to befriend me or to spend time with me. I have never been so lonely. Yet, paradoxically, because I lived alone, I was finally able to face my loneliness. I cried and cried for days when I was not in a meeting."

Elizabeth began to witness to a man she met at work and she led him to the Lord. She sought help from the Assembly in discipling him and was rejected. Eventually she had a brief, but guilt-ridden affair. Then she had an affair with another man. Her self-image changed. "I felt good about myself. I grew ten years in six months. Every Christian man I had ever met treated me worse than this non-Christian man I eventually married."

After Elizabeth and her husband moved to California, she began to think again about her relationship with God. "One day I got on my knees and asked God to restore me. I knew I had sinned and was separated from God. So I came back to God and renewed my walk with him. I thought, 'I'm going to make my life right with the Assembly and go back into fellowship there.' I convinced my husband to go with me to a Sunday afternoon meeting.

"It was upsetting that no matter where I was or what Assembly I visited in California, there would be somebody who knew me from Chicago. They would come up to me and say, 'Is this the man whom you had the affair with?' or 'Are you really back with God?' They were asking these questions in front of my husband, who I hoped would come to Christ through these people who were supposed to be so godly.

"When I looked at some of the people in the group, they didn't look happy. They seemed very rigid. I realized that they were still holding things against me that had happened years before. I was beginning to feel uncomfortable again. While we were in California, I attended off and on for two years, but I felt pulled down every time I went. No one reached out in kindness or friendship to us while we were there, not even to go out for a cup of coffee."

AN INTIMIDATED LIFE

Elizabeth's weight problem became more serious. "I became bulimic, so I went to a Christian counselor. I also began to have violent nightmares about the Assembly. The dreams were about things that had happened to me while I was in the group but I had repressed. I had forgotten much of what had happened to me in Illinois. Those memories surfaced after some counseling.

"I remembered that in the Assembly they had treated me as if I weren't fully human. I began to weep for my lost youth and how I had let someone take over my life, how I had allowed people to become so entrenched in my life that it wasn't mine anymore. I was angry that I had to be brought to the point of sinning with a man to have my eyes opened and see that I had been deceived, hurt, and used.

"I have tried to put the pain behind me. I finally decided that I have to enjoy my husband and daughter, enjoy the life I have now. I lost a lot of my life. I always think about what could have been.

"I feel sorry that there are Christians right now living that kind of intimidated life. If you want to go to meetings twenty-four hours a day, you should be able to, but no one should intimidate you into going. If you are too sick and too tired, God is not keeping a scorecard. God is not saying, 'She fell asleep in meeting—she's out of the kingdom.'

"You should never be in a church or fellowship where you have no time to think. Nowhere in the Bible does it say, 'Thou shalt have crowd control or mind control. You shall all walk alike and talk alike.'"

Elizabeth noted that she and others left the group after they had had time away from the constant activities due to illness. "I didn't have any real doubts until I stopped living in the community and wasn't watched all the time. I had time to think.

"I suggest to people who are still part of a group like the Assembly to take a hard look around and ask yourself some hard questions. When people there talk to you, is it always negative and critical? Are you intimidating another person so that you will feel better? Instead of demonstrating care and compassion, do you have intimidation sessions? If people are constantly putting you down, that is not being holy.

"Now I have hope in my life. I have a desire for a future and a tomorrow. I don't want everyone tearing me down all the time. Maybe that is why I am afraid to go back to Christian fellowship. I don't want to go through all that again. When you leave a church, you should not be made to feel like you are committing spiritual suicide. You have to break all ties with the rigid lifestyle. God wants us to put holiness in our lives, not rules and regulations.

"I feel as if I am missing a spiritual hormone. I feel sad because my husband and child need me to be strong so that they can come to Christ, but I am a spiritual invalid. The Assembly promised closeness to God, but the end was spiritual confusion."

As a result of that spiritual confusion, Eric Wilson, Melodie, and Elizabeth Walsh had to struggle long and hard to find true freedom in the Christian faith.

Perhaps the freedom these former members now experience is best represented in Christmas. Melodie had told me, "The Assembly doesn't celebrate Christmas or other holidays. Members are kept from their families on those days by being kept busy on outreaches during those times. The children of members wonder why their parents are going to Juvenile Hall on Christmas to cook dinner for the kids there, or enact a Christmas play and make a gift with them and then refuse to celebrate Christmas at home. They see the hypocrisy."

When Eric Wilson told me about his children, he said, "We still don't celebrate Christmas. I told them, 'Next Christmas, we'll get a tree. We will celebrate Christmas.'"

6

A Broken Bone
That Heals Is Stronger . . .

Breaking away from an abusive religious group is a process that usually hinges on a turning point, a decisive event that compels a member to move from doubt to action. For Betty Donald, the turning point came while she was in Haiti as a short-term missionary for the Church of Bible Understanding.

COBU, as the group is often referred to, is a communal group residing in a number of houses in the northeastern United States. The founder and leader is Stewart Traill, who claims that God speaks directly to him and that he is the sole possessor of the correct method of interpreting and understanding the Bible.

The orphanage in Haiti where Betty was serving took in a seven-year-old boy who was very sick and would die unless he had an expensive operation. Betty was anxious: All the short-term missionaries except her had been recalled to the States because of COBU's tight finances. But she called the headquarters in New York City anyway, explained the desperate situation, and asked for money to pay for the surgery. She was told, "Haven't you seen God come through for you before? He'll do the same for you now; trust him."

"Needless to say," Betty recounts, "they never wired money. I sold surplus cooking oil to pay for medication and food. As I was doing that, a Bible verse kept haunting me: 'I have never seen the righteous forsaken or their children begging bread.' I kept thinking to myself, 'If God promised that his children wouldn't beg bread, why am I having to do it?' I knew that my name was tarnished back in the U.S. because I was complaining about the financial situation. At that point, I really didn't care anymore. Everyone was always afraid of what Stewart would think about a matter or say about us. I was sick of the way the group operated."

Betty finally got the boy admitted to a hospital by signing a statement that COBU would cover the bill in full. Then she went to New York and, failing again to obtain funds from COBU, raised the two thousand dollars that was needed on her own. She never saw the boy again, however, because he died in a fire at the hospital.

"I was devastated for weeks after that. At first I was filled with anger, first toward Stewart and then toward the others I knew who compromised and avoided the truth so they wouldn't get dealt with. The result was this little boy's death."

Betty's dissatisfaction was heightened by another event that surrounded the boy's surgery. Along with trying to obtain money from the headquarters, she issued an appeal for blood donors over a Christian radio station in Haiti. "The response was tremendous. I had an opportunity to interact with Christians outside of COBU and found them to be quite sincere. I was surprised at how they worked together and how genuine they were."

After the boy died, any remaining loyalty Betty felt toward COBU died also. "I had to face how dishonest and dysfunctional members were because of fearing what Stewart would say about any type of situation out of the ordinary, especially if it involved spending money. We would try anything possible to avoid being accused of doing something wrong. I had always hated living like that, but would often justify it and hope that it would never result in something serious. This time it did, and I was left to face just how much I'd compromised, justified, and blamed myself for how mean, controlling, and unreasonable Stewart really was. I felt nothing but contempt for Stewart and the organization that I had once been totally loyal to."

PICKING UP THE PIECES

After returning to New York, Betty discovered that a number of changes had taken place in the COBU organization—none of them, she felt, for the better. Stewart was changing some of his teachings, the communal housing in Brooklyn was deteriorating, and several women who were at wit's end were thinking about leaving. In one major group meeting, Betty stood up and publicly denounced Stewart's view of women. Soon afterward, she and two friends laid plans to leave the group. They tracked down an apartment through want ads; because they had not lived on their own for many years, "we all felt bad, a little scared, and excited."

When people finally make the break with abusive churches, they often go through a stage of emotional euphoria. They experience spiritual as well as psychological and personal freedom. Betty cherished her newfound freedom. "I enjoyed going to the grocery store. I felt exhilarated walking in a clean neighborhood with the sun shining. The idea of truly being free was so fantastic. I felt like a freed hostage enjoying life again."

But leaving the group also caused the women to feel insecure and lonely. "We were all shattered," Betty relates, "and trying to pick up the pieces of our lives as best we could. When I first left, I felt as if I were walking around with a dirty secret that only these friends knew and could relate to. It was extremely hard to talk with anyone about my experience, even my family. I wanted desperately to tell my parents everything, but at the same time I was afraid and felt ashamed. I feared that if I told them my story, they might be hindered from coming to know Christ.

"It bothered me greatly that I couldn't relate very well to other people and in fact had very little to say, because the only thing I really wanted to talk about was what had happened to me. My fellow ex-members often criticized my bitterness. I was bitter, of course, because I had been put down and criticized for years."

During Betty's period of doubt in the exit process, she found refuge in renewed contact with a friend, Nancy, who had left COBU four years earlier. "I talked with her weekly, before and after leaving the group. Nancy helped me a lot. She listened to me and helped me work through my questions and doubts without giving a lot of advice. The best thing Nancy did for me was to reflect on her experience and listen without criticizing me."

Once on her own, Betty decided to seek counseling through an evangelical church, but, being still unsettled in the world outside COBU, it was difficult to make a connection. When the pastor failed to keep the first appointment, Betty ended up talking with a deacon at the church for five hours, telling her story for the first time. "I never felt so free and relieved as I did after those few hours."

Eventually she began to receive counseling from the pastor, and by the end of her third session, she began to trust the pastor. "He took a group of about twelve of us to dinner after church one evening. At one point he commented, 'I had no idea what you women had been through.' That comment and others like it, coupled with his obvious concern and kindness, helped me a lot and let me see that some pastors, at least, are approachable.

"Gradually I became more comfortable talking with others about my experience, and I found that the more I talked, the better able I was to sort out my feelings about COBU. I have since made many new friends, have taken up bicycling and aerobics and have been involved in the Singles ministry at my church. But I admit that I still become angry and feel cheated that I threw away a college education because of Stewart Traill. I feel inadequate around others my age who have a career, a home, and a family to raise."

LEARNING TO ENJOY LIFE

Margaret Griffin's recovery process took longer than Betty Donald's. A member of the Church of Bible

Understanding for ten years, Margaret was unable to talk openly about her experience until she had been out for seven. "It is very hard to recover after being violated in an area of one's life that touches the core of our very being. I still have many scars, although I have a sense of wholeness in the Lord that I didn't have seven years ago."

Margaret joined COBU as a teenager trying to cope with the death of her adoptive father. A decade earlier she had been deserted by her natural parents, which left much bitterness and low self-esteem. "The church started out okay, but, due to my immaturity—spiritually and age-wise—I did not recognize some of the warning signs that were there. It took ten years and the spiritual life in me dwindling down to a dimly lit burning wick before I took the hint. On the surface things seemed healthy. Then we became a radical Christian commune, trying to pattern our lives together after the early church in the book of Acts.

"I went through years of public humiliation at the meetings, cramped living conditions, and an environment in which women were treated as inferior to men. I ended up on the street with ten dollars to my name and nowhere to go.

"The Lord has put some beautiful Christians in my path since that time who have loved me and not treated me like a freak. Today I am wiser, and I feel stronger and better equipped than the average Christian who has not gone through this kind of experience. I can 'smell' legalism long before the average Christian can. It's like they say, a bone that is broken is stronger after it has been healed than if it had not been broken at all.

"I have learned since leaving that we don't need to be doing overtly spiritual things to be serving the Lord, although I admit that I'm probably one of the most rigid people I know. But I'm getting better all the time. I've loosened up! People I knew back in COBU days are surprised to see that 'Sister Holy Face'—my own nickname for me during that time—has started to learn to enjoy life."

Both Betty and Margaret had experiences after leaving COBU that sound familiar to sociologists. There is an identifiable set of dynamics at work in the process of leaving a role, whether the exit is from an authoritarian, control-oriented religious group or a place in secular society. Helen Ebaugh explores these dynamics in her book *Becoming an Ex: The Process of Role Exit.*

> Disengagement from old roles is a complex process that involves shifts in reference groups, friendship networks, relationships with former group members, and, most important, shifts in a person's own sense of self-identity.[1]

The exit process involves discarding one's self-identity central to one role and establishing a different identity according to a new role. We can see from many of the case histories presented in this book that, especially for long-time members, the individuals' sense of identity—their badge of belonging—is deeply embedded in the abusive church or organization to which they had committed themselves. When they leave the group, disassociating from their previous role and identity is difficult because of the residual effects.

THE FOUR STAGES OF ROLE EXIT

Dr. Ebaugh has identified four major stages in the role-exit process, regardless of what that role is.[2]

The first stage occurs when people begin to question and doubt their commitment. Doubts usually come gradually and may be related to a number of factors, primarily changes in the organization, disappointments in relationships, burnout, or specific, triggering events.

> Very rarely does [leaving a role] happen as a result of a sudden decision. Rather, role exiting usually takes place over a period of time, frequently originating before the individual is fully aware of what is happening or where events and decisions are leading him or her.[3]

The reactions of friends and other valued people to one's expressions of doubt are crucial. If the initial doubts receive positive social support, there follows a second stage, during which the person begins to seek and evaluate alternatives. Betty's contact with Nancy served this purpose. Assurance from others that the doubter isn't really "crazy" for considering leaving usually accelerates the process. There is a sense of relief at knowing that one is not trapped permanently in the present role but has freedom to choose. The person may begin to imagine how he or she would fit into a new role.

This leads to the third stage, which Ebaugh calls "the turning point," a firm and definite decision to leave. That decision usually comes in connection with a specific event. It crystallizes one's doubts. It can be the proverbial straw that breaks the camel's back.

The turning point usually results in the person's announcing the decision to other people, some of whom may then facilitate the exit. The person may feel relief and a sense of freedom, but also uncertainty and anxiety. The process of adjusting is easier for those who have kept some ties or built some bridges with life beyond the role, such as jobs, families, or outside friends.

The fourth stage is creating and coming to grips with what Ebaugh calls the "ex-role." Relationships are central. The person has to adjust to changes in his or her intimate relationships and friendship groups. An ex-member of a religious group, for example, must deal with the labels and stereotypes that follow him or her.

> One characteristic unique to the ex-role is the fact that exes once shared a role identity with other people, many of whom are still part of the previous role. In addition, there is usually a cohort or aggregate of other exes who have left the previous group. Exes are faced with the challenge of relating to former members as well as other exes.[4]

For people who leave abusive religious groups, the relationship to former members seems to be especially significant. Many of the people I have interviewed for this book have attempted to maintain contact with other ex-members through informal support groups or ordinary social activities. Ex-members are sometimes able to reestablish broken contacts simply reading the organization's newsletter and learning of church-related events that their long-lost friends might attend.

A good example of this kind of networking is the San Francisco-based KIT Information Service, which sponsors annual conferences and publishes the monthly *KIT (Keep in Touch) Newsletter* for former members of the communal Bruderhof society and the Hutterites. The service also publishes annually a directory of ex-member addresses. The newsletter consists mainly of letters written by former members of the Bruderhof, but also contains news and information about the society, book reviews, and ex-member reunions.

Ramon Sender, the editor of the *KIT Newsletter*, directs his comments to the current leadership:

> So, Bruderhof folks, I would suggest that instead of labeling ex-members as "unfaithful," you should see us as your Bruderhof graduates, people who have "served their time." We learned some valuable skills and now are strong enough to test ourselves outside the communities, strong enough to rely on our own feelings and our own consciences, no longer needing the Bruderhof support system to know right from wrong. We peregrines no longer sit captive and hooded in a gilded cage. We have unfurled our wings in the wider, more adventurous skies of the outside society. Hey, guys, we're your successes, not your failures! C'mon out and join the crowd! It's not as bad—we're not as bad—as you've been told.[5]

Former members of abusive groups find the same kind of mutual support in their informal gatherings that members of Alcoholics Anonymous (AA) experience. Recovery is largely a group phenomenon. It is difficult to accomplish in isolation. Self-help or recovery groups offer an opportunity to listen to the stories of other spiritually abused people and learn from their experiences. The groups provide a context for gaining insight into one's own issues and motivations. Like members of AA, refugees from abusive churches need an atmosphere of unconditional acceptance. A nurturing group can help victims of spiritual abuse to learn to trust others again. Most important, a support group—whether formal or informal, large or small—provides a sympathetic audience of people who have "been there" too.

SEEKING COMPASSIONATE CHRISTIANS

One additional factor enters into the exit process for many people leaving religious groups. Like others mentioned in this book, Margaret found an attitude among some evangelical Christians to be an obstacle to her recovery:

"When I first left, I didn't find a lot of Christian people who were willing to be compassionate and nonjudgmental toward me. Many churches distance themselves from people like me, and I learned early that it was best to pretend as if I never went through anything like this so as to be treated normal. I think they acted that way mostly out of ignorance and fear. Now that I have been able, with the Lord's help, to deal with my experiences, I can speak openly. But it surely would have helped back then, when I was hurting and alone, if I had seen a different attitude demonstrated by people whom I met in the Christian community at large.

"Our Lord is faithful, and there were a few Christians who could see past the church I had been in and who could see that I knew the Lord but had been battered—like the man the good Samaritan rescued— and needed a huge dose of love."

Margaret feels that now she is on her way to a wholesome recovery. "Last summer we held a reunion of ex-members of COBU. It was really a good experience because we were reminded of the good that had been between us, while at the same time there was healing, enabling us to deal with some of the abusive things that happened in our life together. I think the hardest thing for each of us is to face our own responsibility for a spiritually abusive situation."

7

"God Took Time to Visit His Lost Child"

"The JP story is a tragic tale of good intentions gone bad," writes a former member of the Jesus People USA.[1] JPUSA ("ja-poo-zah"), as it is commonly called, is a Christian community founded in 1972 in inner-city Chicago. It ministers to the poor and the elderly and operates a Crisis Pregnancy Center in the Uptown section of the city. It is perhaps best-known to the evangelical world through two highly visible ministries, *Cornerstone* magazine and REZ, a Christian rock band. JPUSA's annual Cornerstone Festival features Christian rock music, conducts seminars on various topics, and draws thousands of young people. In 1989 JPUSA joined the Evangelical Covenant Church. A council of nine elders-pastors presides over the community of about five hundred members.

There is a side to the JPUSA story, suggested in the opening statement, that is largely unknown. I became aware of problems in the group after receiving letters and phone calls from former members who had read *Churches That Abuse* and saw parallels with their own experiences. The pain and frustration they expressed point to a long-standing pattern of abuse within the organization that cannot be denied, despite some evidence of amelioration in recent years.

LOOKING FOR COMMUNITY

One former member, whom I will call Alan Kaufman, joined the Jesus People in 1971, when the group was still a traveling ministry and had not yet settled permanently in Chicago. He and his brother, both teenagers and new Christians, were attracted to the group by the Resurrection Band. He is now in the counseling profession and states that his experiences in JPUSA help him to empathize with his clients. "I have worked through things that were difficult and painful, and that process has given me a greater understanding of myself and of my God and an inner strength.

"I come from a dysfunctional family—an alcoholic father and a codependent environment. I was a troubled child, forever seeking who I was and trying to find my place in life, more so than the average adolescent. For the three years before I became a Christian, I was involved in the occult, which contributed to my emotional and spiritual instability."

A background like Alan's is common among people who find themselves in abusive church situations. Many join religious groups looking for focus for their lives and looking for community as a place to find themselves. In the book *Community and Growth*, Jean Vanier remarks on the appeal of a Christian communal environment: "Coming from the insecurity of broken families or from families where there is lack of warmth and love, young people are in desperate need of communities where they can refind their deeper selves and experience values that give meaning and a certain structure to their lives."[2]

"One of the first things I noticed was the rules," Alan relates. "It was a communal ministry, and they imposed strict regulations which included limited conversation between men and women, appropriate dress, no television, radio or newspapers. We were cut off from all outside media with the exception of tapes of approved Bible teachers. In the beginning the ministry was actually a discipleship training school with daily classes, hours of prayer and group worship. I enjoyed those, and I believe they were a foundation for my Christian life today."

Alan soon began to question some practices of the group "such as the increase in heavy-handedness." The Herrin family assumed the leadership, and, Alan reports, "With the new leadership, I began to see a new agenda develop.

"We were told to solicit donations, something I had a problem with. *Cornerstone* newspaper was small at that time. We hit the streets, sometimes twelve hours a day, five days a week, to witness, to pass out literature and to ask for money. I seldom came home with more than four or five dollars and a lot less on some days, and I was reprimanded continually for my lack of support. I began to fall out of grace with the leaders at that point.

"My brother had become an integral part of the ministry because of his musical talent, and we were very close. The leaders saw this, and they disapproved. They said that we were too much alike, and they requested that we not spend anymore time together. We were separated and isolated from the familial support we could have drawn from each other. They kept us apart, and I found that to be most hurtful.

"I am a guitarist, and my guitar privileges were taken away from me. I was accused of being possessed by a demon of music. Over time, most of my recreational privileges were taken away, and I began to rebel. I was bucking the system because I didn't like what they were doing and didn't feel it was necessary for them to take from me all the things that were important to me. That is where I believe the emotional abuse began to set in.

"I had my faults and was guilty of many things. I was rebellious in many ways, but I was an adolescent. I was growing up into young adulthood, and the freedom to explore boundaries was not afforded me. They thought I should mature and stand as an adult even though I was an adolescent. Skipping that very difficult and necessary transitional period in life was impossible and absurd. I told them that, and I was reprimanded for being rebellious and unwilling. I was not permitted to fully participate in the ministry."

Alan and other former members testify that at one point the rod was administered as discipline to both adults and children in the community. "The combination of the spanking, the belittlement, the emotional isolation, the familial isolation, and the various desensitizing methods that JP used resulted in the hurt I experienced. I don't know if the leaders were even aware of what they were doing most of the time, that they were taking parts of my life away from me." (The use of corporal punishment with children has diminished, and the practice of adult spanking was abandoned many years ago by the community.)

"YOU CAN NEVER GO BACK HOME"

A disagreement over music with Glenn Kaiser, one of the elders, was the last straw. It was "one of the final verbal blows I took from him. I was frustrated and angry. I felt stifled, and I was struggling. So I approached the elders about leaving. They sat me down and began an interrogation process. The questioning turned to accusations, and accusations to condemnation. They said that if I left JP, I would amount to nothing; I would backslide and go to hell. I was stunned.

"Dawn Herrin took me aside and said, 'If you leave here, you will always be a boy. You will never grow up. You will never amount to anything. You can't leave here; this is where your life is.' I was thinking to myself: this is where my death is.

"I left those two encounters reeling. I couldn't sleep or eat, and I lost weight. I was very distraught. Finally, after much thought and prayer, a friend and I decided to run away.

"I felt strongly that for a person to be effective in the kingdom of God, he must be released when he left a ministry. Before I left JP, I asked the elders to release me. I needed to be released in the Spirit and in love and to be blessed. They would not do that. They flatly refused. That really hurt me.

"I stayed at another Christian ministry in Florida trying to find some solace. I was confused, the walking wounded. While with the people in Florida, I had what was one of the most intimate and beautiful experiences with God that I had ever had in my life. I couldn't sleep; I was in pain. About three o'clock in the morning, I got on my knees and prayed for the Lord's direction. All of a sudden, the room lit up. I can't describe it. I felt that God had entered the room, and then I felt something inside which I can only describe as the deepest hug I have ever felt in my life. It was hugging my being and holding me. I wept more deeply than I had ever done in my life. I felt loved in that very intimate moment. Almighty God reached down to one of his lesser children and told him that he loved him. I also felt in my heart that he had asked me to go back to JP and make things right. A week later, I went back to Chicago.

"I humbled myself before the leaders and asked them to forgive me, which was perhaps the hardest thing I have ever done. There is an old saying that you can never go back home. That is very true. After two months back at JPUSA, I was still questioning the motives of the leadership. I could not agree with how they were handling people or finances. I was very critical of what they were doing. I could not and would not buy into it. Instead of accepting me back and working with me in a healthy way, they subjected me to more submission. I was always being watched and having to disclose my thoughts.

"One time I was talking to Glenn, which was difficult to do, about why I left. I told him that I had been a Christian for many years and didn't feel that I had left with any bad motives. He stopped me and said, 'You've come back. You were never saved before. You are saved now. Forget about the other times. You are just beginning.' I felt violated after that, and that was when things began to fall apart for the second time. I knew it would not work. It added insult to injury.

"When someone takes away all that is precious to you and all that you know to be true, and throws it in the garbage can and says, 'No, you were never saved, but now you are,' he is playing God.

"My own brother would not even listen to my case, so I went before the elders again. 'I have apologized and made amends with you about the way I left before. Will you please release me in the Spirit to go and be productive in the Lord?' I asked four different elders, and each one of them denied me that. I was devastated. So I left again, feeling cold, miserable, hurt, and alienated."

SET UP FOR FAILURE

"I constantly moved to avoid stopping long enough to settle down, to allow my mind to hear the message again: 'You will never amount to anything. You'll never grow up. You will always be a failure. You will backslide and go to hell.'

"JPUSA didn't help you deal with aspects of sexuality, resentment, and anger. There was a lot of suppressing and repressing of feelings in the organization. Members had no privacy and no room for failure. Failure is a part of life and a part of our Christian life. It is the proper dealing or improper dealing with failure that makes the difference. When a person does not help you deal with failure of any kind, he is hindering you.

Someone who is not free to share his feelings will mask it, cap it, or hide it, but it won't evaporate.

"I think that many people who leave an abusive ministry experience some of that as well. Initially they show the signs of one who has lost a loved one; and *they* are the loved one that was lost. They go through a natural grieving process, but many of them don't follow through. They stop at the point of resentment and anger at the loss. Subsequently, they gravitate to their old lifestyle. They have nothing and don't look to the future. The past is shot, and the present is nothing but directionless groping.

"I was caught in that for a short period of time, but I did deal with my anger in a healthy fashion. I got a visitation from God, which I think is rare and unique in life, and I am very blessed and fortunate to have had that happen. God took time to visit his lost child who was floundering, and he put me back on the right road.

"But people who could not get the support they needed were at a stalemate and couldn't move backwards or forwards. I have talked to people who left years after I did, and the first thing out of their mouths is anger because of what the ministry did to them. They must deal with that unresolved anger.

"The anger and rage you feel when you realize that you have wasted all those years, that you have been robbed, broken down and used, is intense. You sold your life only to be dumped, kicked out, and given the bum's rush.

"I could have been a statistic of one who is burnt by a church and left to wander aimlessly and drop out of the Christian faith. But I had tenacity and stamina. I looked not to man, but to God."

ROOM FOR THE GRACE OF GOD

Many of the former JP members I have talked with have moved beyond anger, but long for an apology or an acknowledgment that they have been hurt. I sense that for them, the lack of an apology is a stumbling block to full recovery.

"You can talk about cures and recovery," Alan says, "but by no stretch of the imagination is it ever easy. There has to be a real willingness on the part of the individual who has left a ministry which has hurt them, to let go and move on. JP doesn't set out to hurt people, but they operate in such a way that if you get in the way, you are run over. There is no room for deviation in the machine. If you do not agree one hundred percent with their agenda, you are out.

"I think I have gained back my objectivity because I have grieved, have been angry and depressed, and have regained my sense of perspective. I now understand that my significance is not based in my release or in their denial of that release. I understand that the grace of Christ is sufficient in all areas and all matters. For me that was the simple answer. For others, it may not be quite so simple. They may need to have further therapeutic intervention or counseling. Some of these answers cannot be simply doled out with quotes from Scripture. Sometimes it takes intensive one-on-one therapy.

"I am a firm believer that there is room for the grace of God. He can miraculously change things, and he has. In my life he did. My formative years were spent at JPUSA, and that did take a toll. But I speak without anger or vindictiveness. I don't want to attack Jesus People.

"When a member leaves an abusive church or is forced to leave, he walks out with virtually nothing. He leaves a part of himself behind; the years he has invested are gone. You need to deal with loss and bereavement, confusion and anger, and finally, acceptance of that loss. Many fail to accept it and move on. They need to understand that their significance is not in what they had, but it is in their relationship with Christ. They have lost a few years, but they have not lost their soul.

"Everybody should have assistance when they leave. No one should have to tough it out on their own. They should seek the assistance of another, one who has regained confidence and objectivity after leaving. Or they should seek help from a counselor who can help them. That is why I became a counselor. I want to be someone who can be there when the time comes."

SLAYING THE DRAGONS

Peter and Tracy Vaughn fought many of the same internal battles as Alan after they left JPUSA. Peter was a member for twelve years, and at the time I interviewed them, he and Tracy had been out five. They struggled with newfound independence.

"I feel very strongly about my independence now as far as interpreting and understanding my relationship with God," Peter relates. "In JP, other people interpreted it for me. It took years to get to that point in my life where I could do it on my own.

"JP does a great job with people who have serious problems, who are immature and lack self-control. The way they help them is by imposing a control. As long as you stay there and follow the rules, you will get better; but only up to a point. Jesus People gets you to the point where you are teachable and not self-destructive anymore, but JP doesn't allow you to take the next step, to mature and become independent of them. They don't give you responsibilities that sit squarely on you. Keep your job, do what you are told, and they will take care of everything else. Some people there are afraid to leave because they are overwhelmed by the thought of being out in the real world alone. It is almost like being in Russia right now, where people don't know what to do with so many choices.

"People who leave JP don't know how to handle their personal finances. Some members haven't seen a checkbook in twenty years. Friends of ours who left didn't know how to do laundry. They threw a circuit breaker and thought they had destroyed the world. We cosigned a car for them, helped them get bank accounts. Very practical things like these can be huge problems when you first emerge from a communal setting.

"The first thing Glenn Kaiser said to me when we talked about leaving was, 'People who leave here don't do well.' Is that a reflection on them or a reflection on me?

"JPUSA is too insecure to allow God to finish the work he began in these people. They have no concept of a Christian community where people are welcomed in and welcomed out, where they can come and grow through the community. JP is blind to that, but they are beginning now to treat people who are leaving a bit better because some of us have come back to 'haunt' them.

"When people leave JP, they *want* to be dependent. They latch onto ex-members because they are used to being dependent on somebody. We have tried to help quite a few people who have left. You have to wean them. You give them the tools of survival and push them out."

Peter still struggles with spiritual confusion. "We have had a hard time getting involved in other churches. We looked at several different denominations. We did join another church for a few years in New England and when we moved back to the Midwest, they threw us a send-off party and gave us a scrapbook. I showed it to a JPUSA pastor and asked him why didn't we get one when we left JP? Why couldn't they say, 'We love you; we wish you wouldn't leave, but we wish you well. Stay in touch'?

"What I am looking for in a church is a place where I can be intellectually honest. I want to ask the tough questions. I have questions that were never resolved when I was a young Christian. I have to find out what I believe, not what others have told me to believe. I'm not going to roll over and play dead ever again."

Tracy also reveals ambivalence about spiritual matters. "I have had to deal with much emptiness since I left. I didn't know how to hear God's voice. I never had to, because I always asked somebody else. I have regrets about how long I stayed there, but I don't regret going there. I did learn about compassion for the poor and getting along with other people.

"I felt guilty about leaving. We both had dreams after we left. In my dreams I was always being bad.

"The crisis point was the third year after we left. I didn't know if there was a God, or, if there was one, why he had permitted these things to happen to us. I got angry frequently. Now I have figured out what I believe, and I don't want anyone to tell me what to do or believe.

I don't want to go to church anymore, and that makes me feel guilty."

Peter concludes, "Some of the things my wife and I have done to make the transition are unorthodox. I had to express my anger in a nonviolent way; I yelled and screamed. I had to confront the personal demons in my life and make the choice to put them behind me. I slew the dragons myself, for me. That was an important step."

DIFFICULT CHOICES

Steve and Bridget are examples of former members who have felt the effects of the JPUSA community on their marriage and their children. Both came to JPUSA as adolescents, and they were married there.

"I lived at JP for fourteen years until last year, when we left," Steve reflects. "I grew up there. We have friends and family there. I don't like what's going on at JP, and I have told them so. I don't want to discard the relationships that are important to us, and that is why I have tried to keep the lines of communication open, but it is difficult. Other ex-members chose to join JPUSA; I didn't, and neither did my wife. We were both sent to JP by our parents.

"Before I came to JPUSA, I had suffered from depression and loneliness, but at JPUSA I wasn't lonely anymore. My dad left us when I was two years old, and my mother was an alcoholic. I felt as if I were nobody. Both my parents were abusive. When I arrived at JPUSA, I felt I really had a family for the first time. A JP pastor and his wife became my foster parents, and their kids are like brothers to me. A lot of the pain I've had has come at their hands, but they were following guide-lines set down by JPUSA. I know what it was like grow-ing up there; many ex-members don't."

Bridget came to JPUSA just after her fifteenth birth-day. "It wasn't my choice to go there. I was adopted as a child and lived with my foster parents for six years be-fore they shipped me off to JP. I was a rebellious teenager, but I had not done anything really wrong, so I don't know why they sent me to JP. I wish they had never done it."

Finding a new family in a controlled environment like JPUSA's is a mixed blessing. The members dis-courage contact with families, saying, "We're your par-ents now, and this is where God wants you." This displacement of parents and family is viewed by Peter Sommer as a crucial problem in groups like JPUSA:

> Eventually all of us must find an identity apart from our family of origin—we must grow up. But . . . the unhealthy group takes a critical step here: rather than moving away from my parents to Christ himself, I move away to the group or its leaders. *This feels like growth. In fact, it is only a trade.* Although the people, places, activities, and vocabulary may all be new and stimulating, growth is not occurring. Dependent chil-dren in fact are not growing into responsible adults—they are transferring dependence to the new authority figure.[3]

Coming out of this over-protective environment, Steve and Bridget felt totally unprepared for marriage. Neither knew much about sexuality, and neither knew the other had been sexually abused as a child. "In JP you are not allowed to talk about your past life when you're engaged. If something happened, we were told that it would take care of itself. What happened years ago is only in the past and you have to deal with what's now and what's ahead. If I had known the truth, I would have postponed the wedding. Our honeymoon was hell—a nightmare. And we weren't even allowed to set our wedding day; they set it for us."

In light of the JPUSA experience, Steve and Bridget say they have a difficult time disciplining their two children. "It is hard to be good parents when you have no models to follow. We didn't have any parents to look up to. It has been a struggle for both of us."

The couple has had a long road back to normalcy since leaving JPUSA. "We go to church," Steve says, "because we know that if we're faithful to God, even if we may not feel him or may not understand it all, he will stay faithful to us. That is why I think we've stayed where we are now. For almost a year we did not go to church at all."

Steve described the environment at JPUSA as "a very mechanical type of spirituality. I told one pastor when we were leaving, 'I'm leaving because I want to be a Christian, but I can't be one here. It's too easy for me to become a machine and just follow the crowd. I'm twenty-five years old, and I'm burned out physically and spiritually. I feel like I'm old. I want to take my Christianity and be responsible for it myself because on Judgment Day, God won't be asking you what happened; he'll be asking me.'"

When Steve and Bridget left, they tried to get help through a counseling group for a while, but it proved to be a painful experience. "We couldn't share a whole lot because we were uncomfortable with a group setting," Steve says.

Bridget responds, "I'm afraid to get to know people and to really open up with them, even one on one. I've been hurt too many times. I can't deal with talking to people. I don't want to meet people. I'm afraid. I don't really trust anybody, even my husband. There are many times I feel like committing suicide because there is so much pain. Everything—marriage, children—happened too quickly. I hate my life. There are times I want to forget about my husband and kids and end it all. Sometimes I want to crawl into a hole and never come out.

"Right now I am trying to figure out where God stands in my life. I have been so ripped off. Do I blame God? Do I blame my parents? Do I blame the ministry? Whom do I blame? I don't know where God is in my life at this point; my walk with God is very uncertain. I am faithful about going to church, but I don't know if I want God in my life right now."

Steve once told Bridget, "I'm not ever going to be normal, and neither are you. We're not going to be normal, average persons. I would have loved to have been in a high school and dated you. I would have liked to have made decisions—the right decisions or the wrong decisions, but they would have been my decisions."

In spite of it all, Steve is optimistic about the future. "No matter what, we are deeply in love with each other. The bottom line is that the only thing we definitely, positively know to be true is that we love each other, that our kids love us and we love them. That is one thing JPUSA didn't give us. They didn't plan on that happening."

8

"Grace Is the Best Thing in the World"

Sociologists look for patterns in human behavior. In this book I have tried to present an "insider perspective" by using a life-history approach to illustrate patterns of spiritual and emotional abuse. The case histories are retrospective accounts presented through interviews that concern a significant phase of these people's lives, namely, the experience of leaving a church or religious group that abuses and the process of recovering from that group's hurtful effects.

Social scientists have long used the life-history approach to probe the subjective meaning of any given situation or series of events in the life of a person. Helen Ebaugh writes, "The basic assumption behind the life-history method is that every person defines the world differently. In order to explain these definitions and relate them to social behavior, sociologists must understand what events mean to the people experiencing

137

them. The subject's definition of the situation takes precedence over the objective situation since, as Thomas and Znaniecki (1927) have argued, 'If men define situations as real, they are real in their consequences.' This means, in essence, that the way an individual perceives an event or situation impacts his or her behavior."[1]

Although I have tried to communicate the emotional pain and spiritual confusion of former members, the reader cannot feel the intensity of the emotions of the people who speak in these pages. Their stories would be all the more powerful if you could hear the quiet sobbing or the painful pause as their interviews brought back memories almost too sensitive to share.

I recognize that some readers believe that "abuse" is too strong a term to use in connection with unhealthy churches and Christian organizations. But I do not know a more adequate concept to describe the constellation of traits that I have identified in this book and elsewhere: the practice of surrendering personal autonomy to an authoritarian group or pastor-leader; the loss of identity and self-worth that accompanies that submission; the temporary and sometimes sustained spiritual paralysis; the recurrent nightmares and flashbacks; the relational disruptions and the fear and confusion caused by a performance-based faith. David Johnson and Jeff VanVonderen also call this abuse:

> There is no test to diagnose spiritual abuse. There are only spiritual clues: lack of joy in the Christian life; tiredness from trying hard to measure up; disillusionment about God and spiritual things; uneasiness, lack of trust, or even fear of those who care about "God" things, even legitimately; a profound sense of missing your best Friend; cynicism or grief

over good news that turned out to be too good to be true.[2]

Whatever label we apply, spiritual abuse is an issue the Christian community must acknowledge and confront. It is far more prevalent and much closer to the evangelical mainstream than many are willing to admit. I received a letter from a woman in the midwestern United States who described her experience as a new believer, attending an evangelical church that she had every reason to believe was "mainstream."

"I could not believe what we had found after our first visit," she wrote. "The genuine love and concern for us, the dynamic preaching of the Word; we just knew we were 'home' to stay."

This woman soon learned that she was in a legalistic, controlling church. "My Christian life became very unsettling. Of special concern was my lack of joy in Christ. I felt that it had been snuffed out. I no longer read my Bible because it thrilled me, but because I was supposed to. Bible study was three times weekly. If anyone missed, they were thought to be 'carnal.' No one was to move away from the church. To do so was to walk away from God, since there was no other church that was preaching the 'truth' like ours. Our daily walk became one of trying to be on top of every sin so that God would not break fellowship with us. One beautiful young girl killed herself because she so desperately wanted to be pleasing to God, but only found failure."

The writer states that she became physically ill with panic attacks and stomach problems. "This church left victims scattered and confused. The good news is that the Lord slowly and gently picked me up from such despair. I now have a church where the pastor leads us to Christ, not to himself. There is a balance that I've never known before, and I'm mending. I have a great hope in my Lord and have experienced his love and provision."

"MENDING" IS POSSIBLE

The message of this book is that "mending" is possible! There is hope. You can trust again. However, it is important to understand that although there are some common aspects to the process of recovery and healing, the route is different and can be more tortuous for some than for others according to their personalities and the special problems they encountered in the church.

Here are some suggestions, briefly stated, that may help smooth the road to recovery.

- For closure to take place, there needs to be an acknowledgment of abuse. Denying what has happened will only stall recovery.
- Find someone who will listen to your story, who supports your desire to gain healing and restoration.
- Talk freely about your experiences, doubts, feelings, and hopes.
- Recognize that you will probably go through a grieving process—grief for the lost years, the lost friends and family, the loss of innocence.
- Expect to feel guilt, fear, and shame. It is crucial to find people who will support and validate your own step of faith and can help you address your hard feelings.

- Expect to feel foolish and experience self-doubt. You may ask yourself over and over, "Why did I let this happen to me?" Feeling foolish and regretful about poor decisions is a sign of growth; you will soon leave those emotions behind.
- You will need to trust again, in stages. Above all, learn to trust God again. Renew your walk with him; rebuild a quiet time; don't give up on the church, despite its imperfections.
- Relax! Enjoy your new freedoms. Take time for physical recreation, art, music, and just plain fun. Thank God (1 Tim. 4:1–5) for all the good things he has given us to enjoy.
- Remember that forgiveness is crucial to recovery. It has been said that forgiveness is for the benefit of those giving it, not for the benefit of those receiving it.

A man who escaped an abusive group with his wife experienced most of the phenomena I have suggested. "Waves of bitterness and hurt would come up occasionally, but the waves of love and new life were stronger. My wife and I grew closer, as we sorted out the bad and good in our experience. There was a lot of good; we needed to learn not to focus on the negative, but to rejoice in our new freedom. Eventually we even began to laugh at some of the things that occurred in the old church. This did serve as medicine as we recovered from the pain of abuse. Talking to other former members and sorting out the hidden lessons of the experience we shared were especially healing."

It is difficult to forgive those who abuse us. Lewis Smedes writes about forgiveness in his book *Shame and*

Grace: "Forgiving is a journey, sometimes a long one, and we may need some time before we get to the station of complete healing, but the nice thing is that we are being healed en route. When we genuinely forgive, we set a prisoner free and then discover that the prisoner we set free was us."[3]

In rebuilding your life you will no doubt benefit from professional assistance, in the form of either pastoral counseling (with someone familiar with authoritarian groups) or therapy. Therapists are trained in a variety of disciplines including psychology, social work, and psychiatry. If possible, select a therapist with a Christian world view who is able to integrate his or her professional practice with a biblical faith. You may want to consider more extended therapy at a rehabilitation center such as Wellspring or New Life Treatment Centers.

TRUSTING IN THE GOD OF GRACE

I conclude with some insights offered by Tami Tucker, a graduate of Wheaton College who formerly directed the Crisis Pregnancy Center operated by JPUSA. Her comments can be applied widely and encompass much that I have said in the book.

"I see the topic of recovery from spiritual abuse in much the same light as I do recovery from parent-to-child sexual, physical, or emotional abuse. All the generalizations I am making are, of course, directly a result of what I see at JPUSA, but I believe these are principles which can be generalized to some degree to spiritual abuse within the church at large.

"You will often hear JPUSA leadership refer to themselves as surrogate parents—probably a residual of the 'shepherding' philosophy which influenced them greatly in the early years and which they still reflect in many ways. What happens is that emotionally damaged young people move from dysfunctional natural families right into dysfunctional church 'families,' and feel completely at home because it is a 'cleaned-up' form of what they've experienced all their lives. It does not violate their sense of order or what I believe are false foundational premises upon which they have built that life. Many of those false premises have to do with the role of authority and the notion of 'submission' as well as the idea that sin is primarily some form of behavior rather than the underlying condition of fallen humanity.

"In the case of JPUSA, the real destructiveness of these false premises and their relation to spiritual abuse can be seen in ways different from a traditional church setting because of the intimacy of the community environment and the group dynamics of a 'damaged' population interacting in that context. This may be one reason why it may be difficult and confusing for someone who has never lived communally to fully understand the implications of dysfunctional community life on an emotionally damaged individual.

"On a more general level, I think the most confusing aspect of religious abuse in our society is that it does not usually occur as an isolated event in a person's life. Emotionally healthy people generally are not pulled into abusive religious cycles and are not paralyzed by the rejection they experience when they recognize problems which exist and leave the church. On the other hand, emotionally unhealthy people will first welcome salvation with open arms because of the deep sense of emptiness and pain in their lives. For these people, fear of rejection, fear of authority figures, and personal insecurities prevent them from leaving a problematic church or even recognizing the problematic elements.

"When some do gather the strength to leave the unhealthy situation, the rejection they receive—especially if their personal relationship with God has become distant or displaced—can cause them to reject or question their original salvation experience and God himself. Marriages crumble under the pressure, and individuals who have a history of substance abuse often go back to the same abusive behavior, or worse.

"My husband and I have seen a number of things contribute toward wholeness, both in our own recovery and in that of others:

1. Twelve Step groups
2. Group or individual counseling
3. A warm, accepting church or small group setting
4. Ex-member support groups

"Recovery from spiritual abuse is similar to other kinds of victim recovery in that deep healing usually occurs within and through relationships with others. People who have been deeply hurt tend to be angry loners, gun-shy, and committed to self-protection. But learning to trust and allowing yourself to become vulnerable to others and to God, by definition, requires relational input."

People recovering from spiritual abuse have a deep fear of rejection, of not being accepted. Experiencing acceptance, whether in a small group or in a caring church, is often the beginning of their healing. It involves, as Tami points out, learning to be vulnerable to others—and to God. In being vulnerable to God we open ourselves to his amazing grace. Lewis Smedes writes, "Grace is the beginning of our healing because it offers the one thing we need most: to be accepted without regard to whether we are acceptable. Grace stands for gift; it is the gift of being accepted before we become acceptable."[4]

God is extravagant with his grace. In Ephesians 1:7–8 the apostle Paul reminds us that the riches of God's grace have been "lavished" on us through Jesus Christ. I have seen "amazing grace" at work in the lives of battered believers who have been restored and "re-created" by the grace and power of the living Christ. Smedes puts it succinctly and well: "I believe that grace is the best thing in the world."[5]

Recovery means trusting in the God of grace, the God of endless years. Remember the promise made to Israel in Joel 2:25: "I will repay you for the years the locusts have eaten."

Epilogue
Can Churches Change?

The testimony of this book is that battered believers can recover. But is rehabilitation possible for churches that abuse? Can a spiritually abusive system be changed? The answer is yes, even though in reality many churches do not experience significant change. Sometimes the modifications are only cosmetic or superficial, perhaps in response to pressures from the membership or out of a desire to gain legitimacy and acceptance from the larger Christian world. Transformation usually comes slowly. The mindset of the typical authoritarian leader is to resist succumbing to calls for change rather than admit failure or weakness.

But some do answer these calls, and as evidence I will cite two groups described in *Churches That Abuse.*

The network known as Great Commission Association of Churches (GCAC) claims that it has taken significant steps in the direction of reform and reconciliation with disaffected ex-members. They have published and circulated a "Statement of Errors and Weaknesses" and have discussed the issues raised in that statement in

147

several elders' conferences. The leadership believes they have made sincere attempts to seek reconciliation with disaffected former members. The group has taken steps to encourage accountability to others and has sought advice from several ministry consultants, including leaders of the National Association of Evangelicals and leaders of Campus Crusade for Christ, concerning the errors and problems of the past. They have also encouraged their staff and pastors to pursue additional seminary training, and they have instituted a Council of Reference, individuals to whom the GCAC leadership can go for counsel.

Dr. Paul Martin, director of Wellspring and a former member of Great Commission International (as the group was formerly called), concurs with the opinions of many other former members:

> Some encouraging reforms have occurred in recent years after the founder, Jim McCotter, left the movement in the late 1980s. However, the current leadership has not yet revoked the excommunication of its earlier critics. The admissions of error so far have been mainly confined to a position paper, the circulation of which has been questioned by many ex-members. Furthermore, Great Commission leaders have not yet contacted a number of former members who feel wronged and who have personally sought reconciliation. There has been some positive movement in that direction, but most ex-members that I have talked to are not fully satisfied with the reforms or apologies and feel that the issues of deep personal hurt and offense have not been adequately addressed.[1]

GCAC leader David Bovenmyer indicated in a letter that "we have not been able to achieve reconciliation

with all, yet our sense is that some of our most severe critics will not be pleased with us unless we fully vindicate
them and join in their denunciations of Jim McCotter,
something we cannot in good conscience do."[2]

A former member sees in such an attitude a pattern
that "protects unequivocally the prophet-leader, keeping him in holy light, irregardless [sic] of the realities
of distortion and problems seen from those not under
the spell. The implication is, then, that they, even though
having made significant moves, are still under 'the
spell.'"[3]

Another group that responded to charges raised in
Churches That Abuse is the Word of God community in
Ann Arbor, Michigan. Well-known in charismatic
Christian circles, the Word of God community exerted
considerable psychological and spiritual influence over
its members after its founding in 1970. In an extraordinary "family meeting" held on June 2, 1991, Ron
Ghormley admitted that the pastoral care system had
major flaws. He mentioned that the system had become
"too controlling," that "immature and dependent
Christians" were often the result of the faulty system,
that people were often treated more like children than
adults, and that the system fostered an unhealthy elitism. Ghormley stated, "We, the leadership of the community, need to repent to all of you and especially to
those who have been hurt by what we all thought and
hoped would be a wonderful approach to achieving a
wonderful Christian life."[4]

According to the *Detroit Free Press,* Ralph Martin, the
popular leader of the Word of God, confessed that the
community's failings included "legalism," "self-impor-

tance," "disdain for other Christians," "secrecy," and "authoritarianism." The *Free Press* quoted Martin:

> The Word of God community began in a genuine en-
> counter with God in the power of the Holy Spirit.
> We wanted to give our whole lives to him and be
> fruitful in his service. To a large extent, this is what
> happened. But . . . a gradual shift occurred which we
> scarcely noticed at first: We moved from primarily
> trusting in and exalting Christ to focusing more and
> more on "our way of life," "our teaching," "our lead-
> ers," "our approach," "our community."
>
> As a leader during this time it's been humbling,
> embarrassing, and a cause for grief to see the differ-
> ent ways we've gotten off the track, and the ways in
> which we've grieved the Lord and our brothers and
> sisters in Christ. It's been a time for repentance, for
> soul searching, and for change.[5]

I have suggested to leaders of the Evangelical Covenant Church that the Word of God community might serve as a model for change in Jesus People USA in view of the testimonies of former members. There has been much correspondence between leaders of the Covenant Church and JPUSA and me since I began to do the research for this book. They have questioned the integrity of my reports, the reliability of my respon-dents, and my sociological methodology, but I have conducted more than seventy hours of in-depth inter-views and telephone conversations with more than forty former members of JPUSA. They have also largely dis-counted the reports of abusive conditions past and pre-sent in the JPUSA community. One denominational official wrote to me in September 1993, "You need to know that we have investigated all charges against the

Jesus People and have found them to be unsubstantiated or false."[6] Another Covenant administrator claimed that the characteristics I had identified regarding JPUSA were "untrue," "misleading," and "unsupported."[7]

JPUSA pastors and Covenant administrators have reconceived my research findings as "accusations," "charges," and "allegations." Unfortunately, this inaccurate redefinition of scholarly research may give some the impression that I am *personally* bringing complaints against a Covenant congregation. It unfairly casts me in an adversarial role, something I reject.

Former members have also confronted denominational and JPUSA officials about their concerns, most notably living conditions within the community, spiritual elitism, authoritarian control over members, the failure to nurture members toward maturity and independence, and the difficult exit process. Repeatedly these members have felt their experiences and concerns were ignored, discounted, or rationalized away. But in late 1993, under the auspices of the Evangelical Covenant Church, a select group of former JPUSA members met with key JPUSA leaders. A mediator from the Alban Institute led this first formal attempt at reconciliation. It remains to be seen whether the process will continue or where it will lead. But one former member present later expressed the hope that it would prove to be "the beginning of the beginning."

Can JPUSA change? Will JPUSA change? There is evidence that some conditions have changed. But there also appears to be an unwillingness or inability on the part of the leaders to admit that serious problems persist.

The December 1993 meeting involving about a dozen former JPUSA members together with Evangelical Covenant Church leaders and JPUSA pastors should not be interpreted as a formal acknowledgment of spiritual or emotional abuse within the community. However, the leaders have expressed some sympathy with the complaint that leaving JPUSA can be a difficult process. They have initiated steps to facilitate departure and subsequent life adjustment for those members wanting to leave.

Significantly, however, the leaders view problems of leaving largely in terms of transition from a communal setting to a noncommunal one. By limiting their concern to practical and utilitarian matters such as securing housing and opening a bank account, the leadership overlooks the painful interpersonal and psychological hurts that often accompany departure. For example, one woman who had been a member for nearly twenty years said that following their decision to leave ("we were told we had sixty days to go"), no one spoke to her husband for weeks. He became, she said, "the invisible man." In a letter to a JPUSA pastor the husband wrote, "Do you have any idea how difficult it has been to adjust? What our kids have gone through? Do you care? As a pastor, can your concern for others reach beyond your agenda? Do you have any idea how it feels to be part of something for so long, and then be treated as if you were never there at all?"

Leadership shortfalls in Christian organizations are not easy to acknowledge, but spiritual wholeness and renewal cannot be achieved until unhealthy behavior is recognized and dealt with. Unless abusive behavior is confronted and confessed, the likelihood of real change is diminished.

Unwilling to admit serious deficiencies and insensitivity in their pastoral style, the leaders of JPUSA have instead sought to discredit the former members who have cooperated with my research efforts. As Stephen Arterburn and Jack Felton remind us, it is often the case that "anyone who rebels against the system must be personally attacked so people will think the problem is the person, not the system."[8]

JPUSA may well be an instance in which a significant distance has developed between the official teaching of the organization and the reality experienced by many rank-and-file members. This is what sociologists describe as the differences between "ideal culture" and "real culture." Leaders may sincerely not recognize that their leadership style and policies are experienced by many members as a spiritual elitism and an authoritarianism that borders on "speaking for God." They do well to regard the words of this former member of JPUSA: "I believe that the leaders themselves have become victims. I have spent a lot of time with some of them, and many really do love the Lord, but I believe that they are deceived themselves. They have no idea how much pain they have caused in hundreds of people's lives."

But JPUSA has also had a wonderful ministry to the margins of society in the inner city of Chicago. The organization has had a positive impact on the Christian world through *Cornerstone* magazine and REZ band. Ironically, though, many of its own members have been marginalized in the interests of "the ministry" and "the community." I pray that through the good services of the Evangelical Covenant Church and the Alban Institute, JPUSA will become a shining example that reconciliation with former members and genuine change are possible.

Appendix
Issues in Recovery

Many themes and issues have emerged from these stories of people recovering from churches that abuse. These are often more implicit than explicit. Thinking through these issues in the following terms may be helpful to victims of abuse and those who seek to counsel them.

WHY PEOPLE ARE DRAWN INTO ABUSIVE GROUPS

- Emotional needs
- The attraction of authority
- False expectations
- The deception of positive impressions and ready acceptance
- Vulnerability through inexperience with a healthy Christian faith and community
- Dependency needs

FACTORS THAT MAKE IT DIFFICULT TO LEAVE AND RECOVER

- A system that fosters dependence
- Members not encouraged to think for themselves
- The community emphasized rather than the individual
- Emphasis on uniformity and conformity
- Social skills undeveloped
- "Set up" to fail: self-fulfilling prophecy
- Feelings of being "orphaned" and rejected
- Culture shock
- Nowhere to turn for faith, because other churches discredited
- Ill-equipped for relationships
- Isolation from society
- Estrangement from family
- Loss of focus and purpose in life
- Feelings of shame and guilt
- "Victimization" syndrome
- Lack of trust in authority and/or intimacy
- Insufficient resources (financial, emotional, relational)
- Feelings of anger and bitterness impeding forgiveness
- Network of friends within the membership

FACTORS THAT MAY RETARD OR INTERFERE WITH RECOVERY

- Feelings about oneself: self-esteem
- Economic instability
- Caution about entering another Christian community or church

- Dependency
- Need for resocialization
- Marital and family conditions
- Need for professional counseling
- Being viewed with distrust or skepticism by other Christians
- Lack of self-discipline
- Spiritual paralysis

SOME FEELINGS TO CONTEND WITH

- Rejection
- Low self-esteem
- Shame and guilt
- Futility
- Isolation
- Inadequacy
- Grief
- Regret for lost years
- Loss of identity
- Fear and confusion

Farewell to Foundry
a poem about leaving j.p.u.s.a.

Hammers falling
louder than words
sword into plowshear
back into sword.

Faith for kindling
fire's stoked
and blacksmiths eat
the chimney smoke.

Iron against spirit
bones against steel
this anvil breaks
more than it heals.

Drench the furnace
forsake this boundary
the mold is smashed
farewell to foundry.

Notes

Preface

[1]Personal correspondence.

One
Searching for Freedom

[1]Juanita and Dale Ryan, *Recovery from Spiritual Abuse* (Downers Grove, Ill.: InterVarsity Press, 1992), 9 – 10.

[2]David Johnson and Jeff VanVonderen, *The Subtle Power of Spiritual Abuse* (Minneapolis: Bethany House, 1991), 20.

[3]Ken Blue, *Healing Spiritual Abuse* (Downers Grove, Ill.: InterVarsity Press, 1993), 12 – 13.

[4]Richard N. Ostling, "Keepers of the Flock," *Time* (18 May 1992), 62.

[5]Kip McKean, "Revolution Through Restoration," *Upsidedown*, no. 2 (1992): 8.

[6]Stephen Arterburn and Jack Felton, *Toxic Faith* (Nashville: Oliver-Nelson Books, 1991), 34 – 35.

[7]Ibid., 35 – 36.

[8]Letter to the Editor, *UpsideDown*, no. 6 (April 1993), 8.

[9]LaVonne Neff, "Evaluating Cults and New Religions," in *A Guide to Cults and New Religions*, ed. Ron Enroth et al. (Downers Grove, Ill.: InterVarsity Press, 1983), 196, emphasis mine.

[10]Ibid., 197. The questions are quoted, but the commentary is mine.

Two
Is There Light at the End of the Tunnel?

[1]Madeleine Landau Tobias, "Guidelines for Ex-Members," in *Recovery from Cults*, ed. Michael D. Langone (New York: W. W. Norton, 1993), 305.

[2]David Johnson and Jeff VanVonderen, *The Subtle Power of Spiritual Abuse* (Minneapolis: Bethany House, 1991), 44 – 45.

[3]Charles R. Figley, ed., *Trauma and Its Wake* (New York: Brunner/Mazel, 1985), xx.

[4]Tobias, "Guidelines for Ex-Members," 313.

[5]Paul R. Martin, "Post-Cult Recovery: Assessment and Rehabilitation," in Langone, *Recovery from Cults*, 203.

[6]Paul R. Martin, "Dispelling the Myths: The Psychological Consequences of Cultic Involvement," *Christian Research Journal* 11, no. 3 (1989): 12.

[7]David R. Miller, *Breaking Free: Rescuing Families from the Clutches of Legalism* (Grand Rapids: Baker, 1992), 34 – 35.

[8]Helen Rose Fuchs Ebaugh, *Becoming an Ex: The Process of Role Exit* (Chicago: University of Chicago Press, 1988), 143.

Three
"I'd Like to Really Live, Not Just Survive"

[1]Stephen Arterburn and Jack Felton, *Toxic Faith* (Nashville: Oliver-Nelson Books, 1991), 247. Perfectionism can become one form of spiritual intimidation. In *Healing Spiritual Abuse*, Ken Blue tells of a young man associated with a Christian organization that stressed the notion that total dedication, sacrifice, and dying to self are essential for spiritual growth. The leadership assigned the young man one degrading job after another in order to "refine his spirit." When he objected to one particular task, "the leaders told him that he was showing signs of rebellion and that he had a long way to go in 'dying to self.' Feeling guilty for once

again failing to measure up spiritually, he submitted all the more to the heavy loads of the . . . leaders." (Downers Grove, Ill.: InterVarsity Press, 1993), 53–54.

[2]Arterburn and Felton, *Toxic Faith*, 228–29.

[3]Ibid., 260, 262.

[4]Interviews have strong therapeutic value, as I have discovered over many years of conducting research. Social scientists distinguish two types of interviews: the therapeutic or clinical interview, the purpose of which is to modify the client's behavior, and the information interview, which is designed to gather data. As a sociologist, I use the latter type. I have found that as I try to balance objectivity with empathy and Christian concern, interviewees are sometimes helped to see aspects of their experience they had not considered before or to sort through feelings they have not confronted. In *Becoming an Ex: The Process of Role Exit*, Helen Ebaugh writes of similar phenomena (p. 217). My point in relating this is that one need not be a psychologist or social worker to make a difference in people's lives. We can be good listeners, come alongside those who have been abused, and point them in the direction of professional counseling.

[5]Paul R. Martin, *Cult-Proofing Your Kids* (Grand Rapids: Zondervan, 1993), 179ff. In this section I rely heavily on chapter 14, "Pitfalls to Recovery."

[6]Peter Sommer, "High Pressure Christian Groups: The Broken Promise," unpublished paper, 1992, 2.

[7]Personal correspondence.

[8]Sommer, "High Pressure Christian Groups," 16.

[9]Ibid.

[10]Martin, *Cult-Proofing Your Kids*, 200.

[11]Arterburn and Felton, *Toxic Faith*, 36.

Four
"Grace to People Who Know They Need It"

[1]Ron and Vicki Burks, *Damaged Disciples* (Grand Rapids: Zondervan, 1992), 5.

[2]Like Miriam, John also testifies that his pre-Christian experience with the Twelve-Step program developed by Alcoholics Anonymous was beneficial for his recovery. Some evangelicals question the value of the Twelve-Step approach for Christians, but others accept it as a complement to biblical counseling. The Minirth-Meier New Life Clinics use it in the conviction that "the Twelve Steps are a pattern for spiritual commitment, growth, and discipleship that every Christian can practice every day of the year" (Sam Shoemaker et al., *Steps to a New Beginning* [Nashville: Nelson, 1993], 15).

[3]David Johnson and Jeff VanVonderen, *The Subtle Power of Spiritual Abuse* (Minneapolis: Bethany House, 1991), 215.

[4]Ibid.

[5]Ibid., 191.

Six
A Broken Bone That Heals Is Stronger . . .

[1]Helen Rose Fuchs Ebaugh, *Becoming an Ex: The Process of Role Exit* (Chicago: University of Chicago Press, 1988), 181.

[2]Ibid., see especially chaps. 2–5.

[3]Ibid., 23.

[4]Ibid., 185.

[5]*The KIT Newsletter* 5, no. 9 (September 1993): 10.

Seven
"God Took Time to Visit His Lost Child"

[1]Shawn Haugh, "The J.P. Experience," unpublished paper, 1990.

[2]Jean Vanier, *Community and Growth* (New York: Paulist Press, 1989), 4.

[3]Peter Sommer, "High Pressure Christian Groups: The Broken Promise," unpublished paper, 1992, 7.

Eight

"Grace Is the Best Thing in the World"

[1]Helen Ebaugh, *Becoming an Ex: The Process of Role Exit* (Chicago: University of Chicago Press, 1988), 31–32.

[2]David Johnson and Jeff VanVonderen, *The Subtle Power of Spiritual Abuse* (Minneapolis: Bethany House, 1991), 194–95.

[3]Lewis B. Smedes, *Shame and Grace: Healing the Shame We Don't Deserve* (San Francisco: HarperCollins, 1993), 141.

[4]Ibid., 107–8.

[5]Ibid., 168.

Epilogue: *Can Churches Change?*

[1]Paul Martin, *Cult-Proofing Your Kids* (Grand Rapids: Zondervan, 1993), 38–39.

[2]Letter from David Bovenmyer, 24 September 1993.

[3]Personal correspondence.

[4]From the text of an unpublished talk by Ron Ghormley, 2 June 1991.

[5]David Crumm, "The Rise and Fall of a Heavenly Empire," *Detroit Free Press Magazine,* 20 September 1992, 18–19.

[6]Letter from Herbert M. Freedholm, superintendent, Central Conference of the Evangelical Covenant Church, 29 September 1993.

[7]Letter from John R. Hunt, secretary, the Evangelical Covenant Church, 30 September 1993.

[8]Stephen Arterburn and Jack Felton, *Toxic Faith* (Nashville: Oliver-Nelson Books, 1991), 260.